# Rise of a New Nation

**Stephen Feinstein**

The Making of America

# Rise of a New Nation

The Chronicle of American History from 1787 to 1815

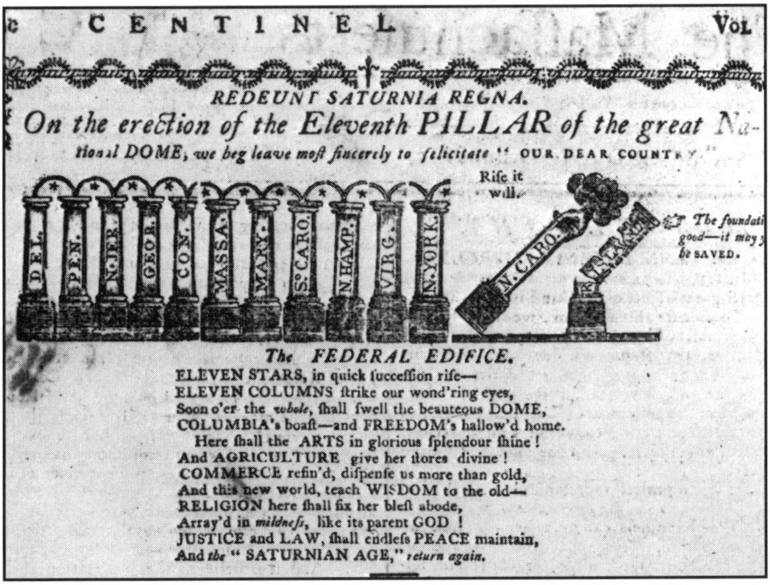

CENTINEL. Vol

REDEUNT SATURNIA REGNA.

*On the erection of the Eleventh PILLAR of the great National DOME, we beg leave most sincerely to felicitate "OUR DEAR COUNTRY."*



*The FEDERAL EDIFICE.*

ELEVEN STARS, in quick ſucceſſion riſe—
ELEVEN COLUMNS ſtrike our wond'ring eyes,
Soon o'er the *whole*, ſhall ſwell the beauteous DOME,
COLUMBIA's boaſt—and FREEDOM's hallow'd home.
Here ſhall the ARTS in glorious ſplendour ſhine!
And AGRICULTURE give her ſtores divine!
COMMERCE refin'd, diſpenſe us more than gold,
And this new world, teach WISDOM to the old—
RELIGION here ſhall fix her bleſt abode,
Array'd in *mildneſs*, like its parent GOD!
JUSTICE and LAW, ſhall endleſs PEACE maintain,
And *the* "SATURNIAN AGE," *return again.*

A Bluewood Book

*THE MAKING OF AMERICA:*
*RISE OF A NEW NATION*
by Stephen Feinstein

A Bluewood Book


This edition produced and published by
Bluewood Books,
a division of The Siyeh Group, Inc.
38 South B Street, Suite 202
San Mateo, CA 94401

ISBN 0-912517-42-5

Printed in USA

Editor: Tony Napoli
Designer: Kevin Harris
Indexer: Kathy Paparchontis

On the cover: A salute to America's new president, George Washington.

*Picture Acknowledgements:*
We wish to thank the following for the illustrations in this book: Bluewood Archives, Library of Congress, Louisiana Historical Society, National Archives, National Park Service, New York Historical Society, New York Public Library, San Mateo Public Library, United States Army, and the United States Navy.

**Stephen Feinstein** is a freelance writer. He has written several books on American political, social, and cultural history. He lives in Marin County, north of San Francisco, California.

Also in *The Making of America* Series:
*Exploration & Discovery (1492-1606)*
*Our Colonial Period (1607-1770)*
*The Revolutionary War (1770-1789)*

Other titles of interest from
Bluewood Books:

*100 African-Americans Who Shaped American History*
*100 Americans Who Shaped American History*
*100 Artists Who Shaped World History*
*100 Athletes Who Shaped Sports History*
*100 Authors Who Shaped World History*
*100 Battles That Shaped World History*
*100 Colonial Leaders Who Shaped North America*
*100 Events That Shaped World History*
*100 Explorers Who Shaped World History*
*100 Families Who Shaped World History*
*100 Folk Heroes Who Shaped World History*
*100 Great Cities of World History*
*100 Inventions That Shaped World History*
*100 Medical Milestones That Shaped World History*
*100 Men Who Shaped World History*
*100 Military Leaders Who Shaped World History*
*100 Natural Wonders of the World*
*100 Scientists Who Shaped World History*
*100 Wars That Shaped World History*
*100 Women Who Shaped World History*

*True Stories of the Wild West*
*True Stories of Baseball's Hall of Famers*

*American Politics in the 20th Century*
*American Business in the 20th Century*
*Media in the 20th Century*
*Law & Order in the 20th Century*
*Technology in the 20th Cenbtury*

# *TABLE OF CONTENTS*

# THE CONSTITUTION STRENGTHENS A YOUNG NATION

On April 30, 1789, General George Washington stood on a balcony of Federal Hall on Wall Street in New York City. Two weeks earlier, the hero of America's victory in the Revolutionary War, had bid farewell to his peaceful and private life at Mount Vernon, Virginia, and, with some reluctance, set out on the 235-mile journey to New York. Now, as Washington calmly took the oath of office as president of the United States, cheers rang out from the crowds lining Wall Street. The throngs of New Yorkers, citizens of the new nation's first capital, had come to witness the first inauguration of a U.S. president.

There had been debate in Congress about what title the nation's leader should have. Some would have been happy to have America become a monarchy, and it would not have bothered them to have George Washington become king. They would have approved of Washington being addressed as "His Excellency," or "His High Mightiness." Indeed, a Senate committee in May, 1789 recommended addressing the president as "His

***Washington's Inauguration, April 30, 1789***

Highness, the President of the United States of America, and Protector of Their Liberties." However, most members of the House of Representatives opposed anything that smacked of a monarchy, even a title such as "His Elective Highness." After all, America did not fight a war to become free of the tyrannical British monarchy in order to replace it with a home-grown version. If the presidency were to be endowed with lofty titles, would a crown, embroidered robe, and hereditary succession be far behind?

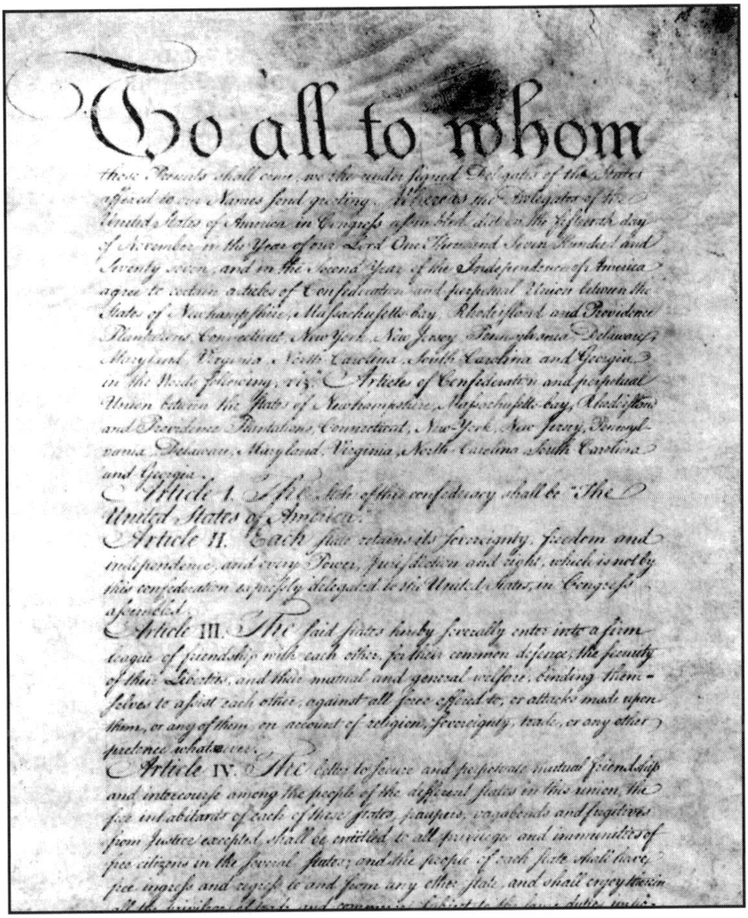

To all to whom these Presents shall come, we the undersigned Delegates of the States affixed to our Names send greeting. Whereas the Delegates of the United States of America in Congress assembled did on the fifteenth day of November in the Year of our Lord One Thousand Seven Hundred and Seventy seven, and in the Second Year of the Independence of America agree to certain articles of Confederation and perpetual Union between the States of Newhampshire, Massachusetts-bay, Rhodeisland and Providence Plantations, Connecticut, New York, New Jersey, Pennsylvania, Delaware, Maryland, Virginia, North Carolina, South Carolina and Georgia in the Words following, viz. "Articles of Confederation and perpetual Union between the States of Newhampshire, Massachusetts-bay, Rhodeisland and Providence Plantations, Connecticut, New-York, New Jersey, Pennsylvania, Delaware, Maryland, Virginia, North Carolina, South Carolina and Georgia.

Article I. The Stile of this confederacy shall be "The United States of America".

Article II. Each state retains its sovereignty, freedom and independence, and every Power, Jurisdiction and right, which is not by this confederation expressly delegated to the United States, in Congress assembled.

Article III. The said states hereby severally enter into a firm league of friendship with each other, for their common defence, the security of their Liberties, and their mutual and general welfare, binding themselves to assist each other, against all force offered to, or attacks made upon them, or any of them, on account of religion, sovereignty, trade, or any other pretence whatever.

Article IV. The better to secure and perpetuate mutual friendship and intercourse among the people of the different states in this union, the free inhabitants of each of these states, paupers, vagabonds and fugitives from Justice excepted, shall be entitled to all privileges and immunities of free citizens in the several states; and the people of each state shall have free ingress and regress to and from any other state, and shall enjoy therein

***Articles of Confederation***

Known as the "Father of His Country," Washington had once again answered his country's call in its time of need. After the Revolutionary War, he had retired to his farm at Mount Vernon in Virginia. There he had hoped to spend the rest of his life, happily managing the affairs of the farm. Instead, he now found himself faced with the daunting task of managing the affairs of the new nation he had helped create. He had a fairly good idea of the immense responsibility that had been placed on his shoulders. Would he be successful, he wondered? Would the American experiment in freedom survive? How could the central government become strong, while at the same time, protecting the freedom of the individual?

In 1781, in the midst of the Revolutionary War, the 13 states had adopted the Articles of Confederation. Under the Articles, the national government consisted solely of a Continental Congress. At that time, the individual states were worried that a strong central government might threaten the rights of each state and limit individual freedom. So the delegates made sure that the Continental Congress would have no power to enforce its laws, and would instead be controlled by the states.

Indeed, the delegates saw the role of a central government as nothing more than a "firm league of friendship." While the Congress was given power in matters relating to the mutual interests of the states such as foreign policy, foreign loans, and the regulation of money, each state retained "its sovereignty, freedom and independence." However, Americans would soon learn that a weak central government had very serious shortcomings.

In spite of limitations to its powers, the Continental Congress was successful in some important respects—it successfully raised an army and waged a victo-

*TEMPERS FLARED UP DURING SHAYS'S REBELLION*

rious war, and in 1783 negotiated a peace treaty with Great Britain ending the Revolutionary War. However, after the war, serious economic problems arose that suggested to some Americans that the time had come to create a stronger central government. Paper money issued by the Continental Congress during the war had now fallen to a small fraction of its former value. In many instances veterans returning home from the war could not collect the pay that was due them. Some who could not pay their debts were thrown into prison and lost their homes.

In addition, as if there were not enough trouble, Britain had begun flooding America with cheap manufactured goods, while at the same time raising tariffs on American goods. However, the states refused to give Congress more power to regulate trade. Indeed, individual states passed trade regulations to their own advantage, and to the disadvantage of other states.

Then in 1786, a situation arose that convinced many people in Congress that they could not afford to wait any longer to strengthen the central government. That year, the Massachusetts legislature, over the objections of the state's farmers, imposed new taxes. Many farmers could not afford to pay, and the courts began seizing their property. When farmers from fifty towns in the western part of the state petitioned the legislature to ease their debt burdens, their plea was ignored. So on August 29, 1786, bands of armed farmers, under the leadership of Daniel Shays, took matters into their own hands. They forced the closing of several courts to prevent further foreclosure of property and processing of debts.

As Shays and his followers continued their rebellious activities in Massachusetts, delegates from five states met in Annapolis, Maryland, on September 11-14. The meeting had been called by James Madison of the Virginia Assembly to discuss interstate commercial disputes that the states could not settle by themselves. At the meeting, Alexander Hamilton, representing New York, called for another convention to be held in Philadelphia in May 1787 to devise a way to strengthen the federal government. The delegates recommended that all the states be called "for the sole and express purpose of revising the Articles of Confederation."

Meanwhile, the situation in Massachusetts grew more dangerous. On January 25, 1787, Shays and 1,200 followers attacked the federal arsenal in Springfield. They were met by a force of 1,000 militiamen under the command of General William Shepherd. Three of Shays's men were killed, and the episode known as Shays's Rebellion was crushed.

Among those Americans who had become alarmed over the rebellion was George Washington. In a letter to James Madison, Washington had written, "What stronger evidence can be given of the want of energy in our government than these disorders? If there is not power in it to check them, what security has a man for life, liberty, or property?"

On May 25, 1787, delegates from all states except Rhode Island arrived at the State House in Philadelphia for the convening of the Constitutional Convention. George Washington and other leading members such as James Madison, Alexander Hamilton, and Benjamin

Franklin were present. Thomas Jefferson, author of the Declaration of Independence, was absent; he was in Paris at the time, serving as America's ambassador to France.

Most of the delegates were Federalists. They favored a powerful federal government and the creation of a new document by which the nation would be governed, one which would ensure the binding of all the states into a unified, single nation. In general the Federalists represented America's wealthiest people, as well as those middle class shopkeepers and farmers who stood to benefit from strong central government control of the economy. The Anti-Federalists were opposed to a new agreement. They were afraid that a strong federal government of and for the elite would threaten the rights of small farmers and others of modest means whom they represented. And so began the drafting of proposals and counter proposals, and the momentous series of debates and compromises on the various plans which would eventually result in the United States Constitution.

On May 29, Virginia Governor Edmund Randolph submitted the Virginia Plan, drafted by James Madison. This plan contained the basic ideas that would become the guiding principles of the new document, and would earn Madison the title, "Father of the Constitution." Representing the large states, the plan called for three equal branches of government—an executive, a judiciary, and a bicameral, or two-house, national legislature, based on the population of the various states. The people would elect members of the House of Representatives, who in turn would elect the members of the Senate. The national legislature would choose the national executive.

On June 15, William Paterson of New Jersey submitted an alternate plan, the New Jersey Plan, which represented the interests of small states. This plan called for a unicameral, or single body, legislature, elected by the people, in which each state would have an equal vote. Debate over the plans raged until

EDMUND RANDOLPH

***WILLIAM PATERSON***

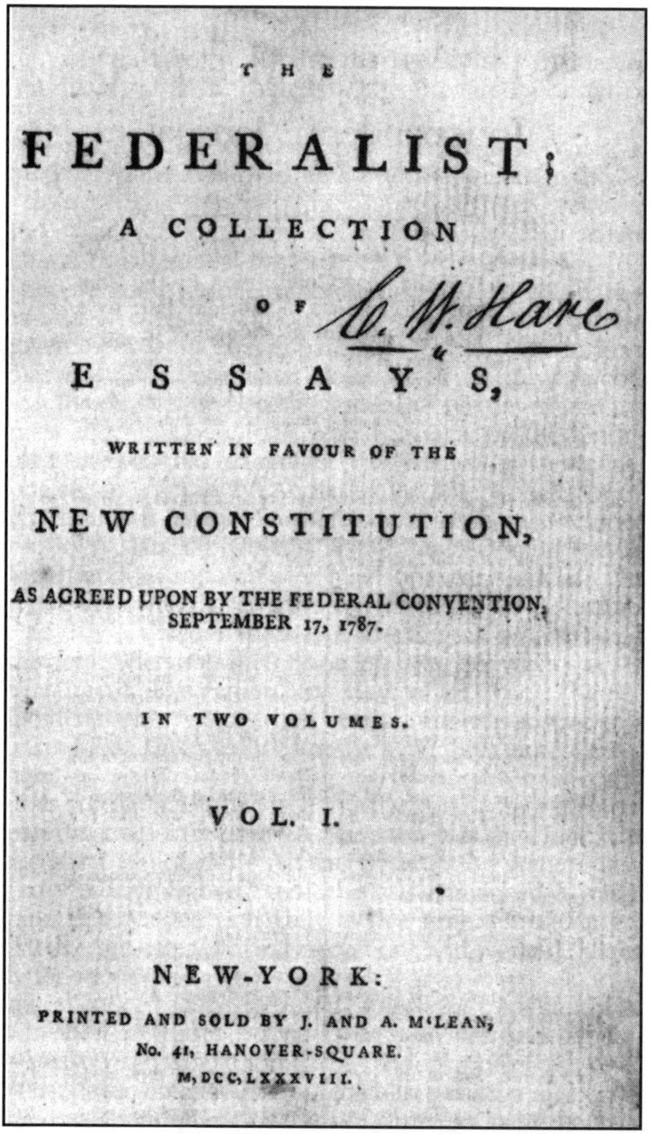

THE

FEDERALIST;

A COLLECTION

OF

ESSAYS,

WRITTEN IN FAVOUR OF THE

NEW CONSTITUTION,

AS AGREED UPON BY THE FEDERAL CONVENTION, SEPTEMBER 17, 1787.

IN TWO VOLUMES.

VOL. I.

NEW-YORK:

PRINTED AND SOLD BY J. AND A. M'LEAN,

No. 41, HANOVER-SQUARE.

M,DCC,LXXXVIII.

**THE FEDERALIST ESSAYS, *PUBLISHED IN 1788***

July 16, when Roger Sherman of Connecticut proposed the "Great Compromise," which called for both proportional and equal representation. The people in each state would elect members to a House of Representatives based on the population of their state, and each state legislature would choose two people to represent their state in a Senate.

The Constitutional Convention ended on September 17, when all but three delegates signed the Constitution. Federalists came away happy that the Constitution specified that federal law would take precedence over state law. James Madison, who had made the major contribution to the Constitution in terms of political theory, reassured Americans that the powerful new federal government would not threaten their liberty because of the separation of powers into the executive, legislative, and judicial branches, and also because of the way power was divided between the federal and state governments.

To promote ratification of the Constitution, Madison, Alexander Hamilton, and John Jay published a series of 85 articles, 29 of them written by Madison, in the New York newspapers under the title *The Federalist.*

The 85 editorials, which were then published as a book called *The Federalist Papers*, made a convincing case for ratification.

***GEORGE WASHINGTON OVERSEES THE SIGNING OF THE CONSTITUTION***

The Constitution was quickly ratified by Delaware, Pennsylvania, and New Jersey. Eight more states ratified it in 1788, one more in 1789, and Rhode Island in 1790. A Bill of Rights would become part of the Constitution in 1791. These ten amendments include the rights of American citizens to a jury trial, protection of freedom of religion, speech, and the press, and due process of law.

On February 4, 1789, electors unanimously chose George Washington to be the first president of the United States. John Adams, who ran a distant second, became vice president. At his inauguration on April 30, Washington swore to faithfully execute the office of the President of the United States, and to the best of his ability, preserve, protect, and defend the Constitution of the United States. In so doing, he solemnly committed himself to doing his utmost to hold the young republic together—to see that the 13 states indeed became a unified nation, rather than a disparate group of individual governments that were continually at odds over economic and political conflicts of interest.

# THE BIRTH OF RIVAL POLITICAL PARTIES

President Washington realized that his goal of building a strong, unified nation was a challenging one. Therefore he knew it was important that he choose for his Cabinet only those with the highest qualifications, individuals with proven abilities based on their service in state governments, or in the Continental Congress or Continental Army during the Revolutionary War. Among the most important of Washington's Cabinet appointments were Thomas Jefferson, the nation's first Secretary of State; Alexander Hamilton, Secretary of the Treasury; and Henry Knox, Secretary of War. Washington also appointed Edmund Randolph as Attorney General, and John Jay as America's first Chief Justice of the U.S. Supreme Court.

*WASHINGTON AND HIS FIRST CABINET*

Washington hoped that his Cabinet advisers would share his vision of where he wanted to lead the new nation. During his eight years in office, Washington and his Cabinet would face a variety of challenges and would have to make many difficult political decisions. Although some of these decisions and certain administration policies would prove to be unpopular with many Americans, fortunately the new nation held together, and was still a viable political entity at the time Washington left office.

Ironically, while Washington managed to maintain a degree of unity among the 13 states, he was far less successful in maintaining unity among the members of his own Cabinet. It became clear early in Washington's first term that his two key Cabinet members—Jefferson and Hamilton—had diametrically opposite views on many important issues, and that in some instances the two would never see eye to eye. Politics always involves compromises of one sort or another, and indeed situations arose in which Jefferson and Hamilton were forced to compromise. However, since the two men of such widely divergent points of view actually represented different constituencies among the electorate, each would eventually find himself the leading spokesman of a new political party.

Hamilton's party consisted of Federalists, and was known by that name. Hamilton's goal was to help the wealthy get wealthier. While Hamilton envisioned an America of big cities and banks, and government-protected industries in which the nation's men, women, and even young children would toil in factories, Jefferson wanted the United States to remain a nation of small farmers and craftsmen, in which government protected the interests of property owners in the South. Jefferson and his followers opposed the policies of the Federalists, believing them to be a threat to the liberties and interests of a majority of the American people.

To counter the influence of the Federalists, James Madison and fellow Virginian John Beckley began organizing opposition to the Federalists in Congress in 1790. In 1791 Madison and Jefferson traveled through New York, Connecticut, and Vermont, meeting with local political leaders and others who shared their views, such as New York

***Alexander Hamilton***

***Thomas Jefferson***

*GEORGE CLINTON*

Governor George Clinton and Aaron Burr, then a lawyer in New York City. By late 1792, Jefferson and others who opposed the Federalists were calling themselves Republicans. They chose this name to show that they supported a "republic," as opposed to the Federalists, whom they suspected of harboring the desire to establish a monarchy in the United States. In fact, some among them referred to themselves as Democratic-Republicans, although Jefferson and Madison believed that the word Democratic sounded too radical! Ironically, members of this party would one day be called Democrats.

Alexander Hamilton, who had said that, "Money is, with propriety, considered as the vital principle of the body politic," was apparently an ideal choice for Secretary of the Treasury. In 1790, the 32-year-old Hamilton was bursting with energy and the motivation to get things done. However, his proposals at Cabinet meetings often met with fierce opposition from Jefferson, and the two would engage in heated debate. At such times, Washington, who favored the Federalist point of view regarding a strong central government, usually sided with Hamilton.

On January 14, 1790, during his first year as Treasury Secretary, Hamilton submitted a plan to Congress for funding the national debt. He believed that America would never prosper unless it got its finances in order, and that paying the debts was "the price of liberty." The Revolutionary War had cost a great deal, and America owed about $12 million to France, Spain, and Holland. There was also a domestic debt of about $42 million, owed to soldiers in the Continental Army and others who had supported the war effort. In addition, the individual states had also incurred debts totalling about $25 million.

According to Hamilton's plan, Congress would create a permanent national debt and assume payment of all outstanding debts, including the debts of all the states. Old depreciated securities would be redeemed at face value and exchanged for new federal government-issued securities whose principal and interest would be guaranteed by a percentage of the national revenue. Just as in Great Britain, the country whose economic system Hamilton admired above all others, merchants would be encouraged to purchase government securities and receive regular interest on them. The merchants would be motivated by self - interest to support the federal government, while at the same time growing

*FIRST BANK OF THE UNITED STATES, PHILADELPHIA*

their businesses for their own and the nation's benefit. Hamilton believed this expansion of commerce would lead to a prosperous America.

Of course, not every member of Congress welcomed Hamilton's plan, nor did they believe the Federal government ought to emulate the British approach to encouraging the expansion of commerce. James Madison argued that southern states such as Virginia, that had already paid off their debts, should not have to participate in the assumption of the debts of northern states, who owed most of the money. It was also common knowledge that as word of the proposed plan leaked out, wealthy speculators bought depreciated securities for very little money, expecting a huge windfall when the government redeemed them at face value. Madison considered such speculation to be immoral. Hamilton, on the other hand, expected that this further enrichment of the wealthy would garner their enthusiastic support of the federal government, and Federalist policies in particular.

Congress debated Hamilton's plan at length and, under Madison's influence, rejected it. Indeed, the House voted it down five times. However, Hamilton wouldn't give up. Realizing that the time had come for some sort of compromise, he met with Jefferson over dinner, and the two talked about their differences over the plan. Then they discussed another issue that had been provoking heated debate—the location of the nation's capital. Hamilton suggested that in return for Jefferson's and Madison's support on the national debt plan, he would persuade members of Congress from New York to vote for moving the capital to a new site on the Potomac River.

An agreement was quickly reached, and it was decided that Philadelphia would become the temporary capital until 1800, while the new "Federal City" (Washington, D.C.) was being built. After Jefferson and Madison produced the necessary southern votes in Congress, Hamilton's plan was finally approved. Later, when Jefferson learned of the full extent of the financial fortune gained by the speculators, he grew angry and bitterly claimed he had been "ignorantly and innocently" misled by Hamilton.

Once the plan for the national debt was decided, Congress passed the rest of Hamilton's program—the creation of a national mint to coin American money, a tax on whiskey, and the creation of a national bank (the First Bank of the United States) to issue paper money and control the nation's credit. Before Congress approved the national bank, however, another debate arose. Jefferson protested that such a bank was unconstitutional since it was not specifically mentioned in the Constitution, and he urged Washington to veto the bank bill. Jefferson, Madison, and Edmund Randolph, in opposing the bank on constitutional

***WHISKEY REBELS TAR AND FEATHER A FEDERAL TAX COLLECTOR***

grounds, became known as "strict-constructionists."

Hamilton, taking a "loose-constructionist" view, pointed out that the bank was indeed constitutional, since Article 1, Section 8 gave Congress power to "make all laws which shall be necessary and proper" to provide for "the general welfare of the United States." Once more, Washington sided with Hamilton. Of course, in Jefferson's view, the bank mainly provided for the welfare of Hamilton's wealthy friends, and its main benefits would go to the North at the expense of the South.

Passage of Hamilton's whiskey tax in 1791 would lead to trouble of another sort—a serious threat, in fact, to the authority of the federal government. When farmers in western Pennsylvania learned of the new tax, they were outraged, and immediately protested its passage. Because they grew more grain than they could eat or transport, they had been using their surplus to produce rye whiskey. The whiskey could easily be sold throughout the region, and indeed could be used instead of money. Over the next few years, the farmers organized against the tax, refusing to pay it. They threatened court officials who tried to collect it, tarred and feathered some of them, and even burned down some of their homes.

When a force of more than 2,000 "Whiskey Rebels" threatened to attack the federal garrison in Pittsburgh in the summer of 1794, the federal government had to act. Washington and Hamilton led a force of 13,000 militiamen to the region to put an end to the rebellion. Apparently, the rebels were so intimidated by the force moving against them that they lost the will to resist further, thus ending their rebellion without a fight.

At the time of the Whiskey Rebellion, Washington had other, far more complex problems to deal with involving America's relations with foreign nations. In 1793, at the height of his popularity, Washington and his vice-president John Adams had been inaugurated for a second term. However, during the next four years, Washington would suffer a serious decline in popularity, largely because of his handling of foreign affairs. And sadly, by the time he left office, many Americans were not sorry to see him go.

In the early 1790s, Washington, Hamilton, and Jefferson agreed on the vital importance to America of trade with other nations. In addition, they all agreed on the necessity of maintaining friendly commercial relations with foreign powers, especially Britain and France. They also believed in the importance of American political neutrality regarding foreign countries. However, when France declared war on Britain in 1793, it became apparent that neutrality meant different things to different people.

Many Americans, including Jefferson, who had served as ambassador to France, had supported the French Revolution in 1789. They believed that the American Revolution had inspired the French, and they rejoiced at the birth of a sister republic. While Jefferson and his Republicans supported neutrality in 1793, in their hearts they sided with France. Other Americans, including Hamilton, believed that America's future economic prosperity depended upon a

***FEDERALIST CARTOON SHOWS WASHINGTON LEADING TROOPS AGAINST INVASION OF FRENCH "CANNIBALS"***

good relationship with Britain. So, while Hamilton and the Federalists also supported neutrality, in their hearts they sided with Britain. The Federalists were especially alarmed at the reign of terror that had descended on France in the wake of the Revolution, and were afraid that a similar chaos could occur in America if the Republicans held sway.

Agreeing with Hamilton, Washington had sought to improve relations with Britain. When war broke out between Britain and France, he followed a policy of neutrality. When British ships began seizing American ships bound for France, Washington sent John Jay, a Federalist with strong British sympathies, to Britain to negotiate a treaty. The Jay Treaty of 1794 settled some issues between the two nations, but many problems remained, including British interference with American shipping, and the impressment of American seamen into service on British warships.

When the terms of the treaty were made public in 1795, there were outbursts of anger throughout the country. Jefferson's Republicans, believing the treaty had been signed at the expense of France, attacked it as "the death warrant of American liberty." Andrew Jackson of Tennessee said Washington should be impeached for signing such a cowardly treaty. John Jay was condemned by many Americans as a traitor for agreeing to a treaty whose terms were so unfavorable to the United States. Yet in spite of all the protests, the treaty was eventually ratified by Congress after much heated debate.

In Washington's farewell address to the nation on September 17, 1796, the new nation's first president cautioned Americans to avoid permanent alliances with other countries and to be wary of partisan politics. Although Washington had tried to rise above politics in his role as president, it proved to be too difficult.

***This Federalist cartoon shows Jefferson tearing down the pillars of government***

Throughout his two terms it had become increasingly clear that there was a sharp and ever widening split along with a growing animosity between the Republican followers of Jefferson on the one hand, and the Federalist followers of Hamilton on the other. Unable to remain above the fray, Washington found himself in the Federalist camp. So on the eve of his departure from Philadelphia, he urged Americans not to allow political parties and the dissension they cause to weaken national unity.

# *JOHN ADAMS AND THE UNDECLARED WAR*

"No! No! Not a sixpence!" said an outraged Charles Pinckney to the three agents of French foreign minister Charles de Talleyrand. Pinckney was one of three American envoys sent to Paris in October 1798 by President John Adams. Their task was to negotiate an end to French seizure of American ships. France, which was still at war with Great Britain, had been infuriated by the signing of the Jay Treaty between the United States and Britain. Because the treaty permitted British ships to continue to confiscate French cargo on American ships, the French had begun seizing American ships bound for British ports.

*CHARLES PINCKNEY*

By the time of Adams's inauguration, France had seized 300 American ships. However, before negotiations in Paris could begin, the French had demanded a bribe from the American envoys. Specifically, the French wanted an initial payment of $250,000 and then a $10 million loan. Furthermore, they threatened to declare war if their demands were not met.

When President Adams learned of the demand for a bribe, he told Congress about it without going into the details, adding that America would now have to prepare for war with France. At this, the Republicans, and even some Federalists, protested that they would not become an ally of Britain against

France. So Adams revealed to Congress what had actually occurred in Paris, and made the information public. The bribery incident became known as the "X, Y, and Z affair," so-called because the three French agents were not named, they were only called X, Y, and Z. When Americans read about the entire account in their newspapers, they reacted with anger.

Almost overnight, most Americans now looked upon France as an enemy. Indeed, the French Revolution and the Jay Treaty had been issues in the presidential election of December 1796, in which Republican admirers of France had campaigned against the Federalist's Jay Treaty. Federalist John Adams, Washington's vice president, narrowly defeated Republican Thomas Jefferson,

***John Adams***

***This cartoon depicts the "X, Y, and Z Affair"***

by a 71-68 electoral vote. Jefferson became vice president, and the administration, split between a Federalist and a Republican, would prove to be a contentious one, and would destroy the friendship that had previously existed between Adams and Jefferson.

Because America now faced a new enemy, Adams's popularity skyrocketed. Angry Americans wanted Adams to declare war on France, and they were ready to march behind him. However, Adams was well aware of America's military unpreparedness, and did not want to risk a French invasion, which a declaration of war might provoke. So he opted for the Quasi-War, an undeclared naval war against France. The nation rallied behind the slogan, "Millions for defense, but not one cent for tribute." Congress revoked all previous treaties with France, and approved a large military buildup including a new U.S. Navy, whose ships were authorized to seize French vessels. Former president George Washington was chosen as commanding general of a greatly enlarged army, with Alexander Hamilton as second in command.

*THE* CONSTELLATION *BATTLES THE* L'INSURGENT

The undeclared war would last for about two-and-a-half years, during which time American ships captured eighty French ships in the West Indies, while losing only one. In one notable encounter, U.S. naval hero Stephen Decatur's frigate *Constellation* captured the French ship *L'Insurgent*. Throughout the undeclared war, Adams came under increasing pressure, especially from the Federalists, to declare war. An ambitious Hamilton, who had been eager to lead an armed force against France, grew particularly angry and exasperated at Adams's refusal to commit the nation to all-out war. Knowing that Republicans would oppose such a decision, Adams sought to rise above partisan politics and steer a middle course. However, even the undeclared war had other consequences that would lead to bitter resentments.

At the height of the anti-France war fever, the Federalist Congress, with Adams's approval, passed the Alien and Sedition Acts. The Federalists, fearing that Republicans might be conspiring with France, wanted to put a muzzle on pro-Republican criticism of Federalist policies. Among such outspoken critics were many recent refugees from Europe. The Alien Acts, of which there were three, gave the president permission to expel aliens whom he considered to be "dangerous to the peace and safety of the United States." The Sedition Act provided fines and jail terms for any person who, among other things, should "write, print, utter, or publish . . . any false, scandalous and malicious writing or writings against the government of the United States," the Congress, or the president.

Although the Alien Acts were never enforced, the implied threats against those with unpopular political views caused hundreds of foreign residents to flee the country. The Sedition Act, however, was wielded by the Federalist Congress as a partisan weapon to stifle any Republican critics. Many pro-Republican newspaper editors and others, including Congressman Matthew Lyon of Vermont, were arrested, tried, and convicted of libel, and sentenced to jail terms.

Jefferson was so alarmed by the Federalists' attempt to limit the Bill of Rights' guarantee of free speech and free press, that he anonymously wrote the Kentucky Resolutions, which were passed by the Kentucky legislature, calling the Alien and Sedition Acts unconstitutional. For similar reasons, James Madison wrote the Virginia Resolutions, arguing persuasively that states had the right to judge the constitutionality of federal laws. Unfortunately, the issue of states rights would later lead to a national catastrophe when southern states used it as a rationale to secede from the Union in 1861.

On September 30, 1800, the United States and France signed an agreement ending the Quasi-War. Never again would the two countries engage in hostilities against each other. Several years after the signing of the treaty, the controversial Alien and Sedition Acts were either repealed or allowed to lapse. However, in the presidential election of 1800, the Republicans would use these Federalist laws as a powerful campaign issue against their rivals.

# THOMAS JEFFERSON AND THE LOUISIANA PURCHASE

President-elect Thomas Jefferson read his Inaugural Address on March 4, 1801, in the still-unfinished capital in Washington, D.C. "We are all Republicans, we are all Federalists," he proclaimed, pleading for national unity. In the election of 1800, the Republican candidates, Jefferson and Aaron Burr, had defeated the Federalists John Adams and Charles Pinckney. However, because Jefferson and Burr each received 73 electoral votes, the House of Representatives had to break the tie and choose the winner. When a group of Federalists decided to support Burr, Alexander Hamilton, who detested Burr even more than he hated Jefferson, argued persuasively against their decision. So thanks to Hamilton's influence, Jefferson became president and Burr became vice-president, and the growing enmity between Hamilton and Burr would lead to tragic consequences.

*THOMAS JEFFERSON*

Jefferson was convinced that his victory in the election demonstrated strong public support for Republican principles. To be sure, his campaign against Federalist attempts to weaken democracy in America struck a responsive chord with the voters. In addition, his ideas about reducing taxes and government spending found favor as well. However, there was another reason for the Republican electoral victory—disarray and conflict within the Federalist party.

When George Washington, who had been planning to help re-elect Adams, died in 1799, Adams lost his staunchest Federalist ally. Then Hamilton, who was angry at Adams because of his peace treaty with France, plotted and schemed with Federalists within the Adams administration to support Pinckney for president instead of Adams. Hamilton had written a pamphlet denouncing Adams as a liar and an ingrate who was "unfit" for the office of president. A copy of the pamphlet fell into the hands of Aaron Burr, who released it to the newspapers. The resulting split among Federalists so weakened the party that the Republicans would control the government for years to come.

*Aaron Burr*

Jefferson drew his strongest support from small farmers in each state, as well as settlers on the western frontier and wealthy southern planters. In Jefferson's view an ideal American nation would be one that consisted mainly of farmers, so he saw the acquisition of new lands as being of the utmost importance for the new nation. The United States already occupied a vast territory, but the population was growing, and new areas for settlement were rapidly diminishing as settlement expanded westward. Unfortunately, the push into new territories often provoked conflict with the Native American inhabitants. Nevertheless, the powerful forces driving the settlement of the wilderness could not be stopped.

According to the Treaty of Paris of 1873, the peace agreement that formally ended the Revolutionary War, the boundaries of the United States were fixed at the Mississippi River on the west, Spanish Florida on the south, and the U.S.-Canadian boundary on the north. France and Spain, the two other European powers controlling territories in North America, had agreed to these terms in the treaty. In the years after the Revolutionary War, growing numbers of American pioneers migrated westward. By the time Kentucky (in 1792) and Tennessee in (1796) had become states, more than one million people had settled there as well as in the Northwest Territory, which would eventually become the states of Ohio, Indiana, Illinois, Michigan, and Wisconsin.

*ROBERT LIVINGSTON*

At the beginning of the 1800s, France controlled a huge territory west of the Mississippi River; known as Louisiana, it included the city of New Orleans near the mouth of the Mississippi. In 1762, during the Seven Years' War between France and Britain, a weakened France had ceded the territory to Spain. But in 1800, the powerful French leader Napoleon persuaded King Charles IV of Spain to cede Louisiana back to France.

For American settlers living west of the Appalachian Mountains, the Mississippi River was the most practical route for shipping their goods. Indeed, the settlers' very existence depended on free access to the river. It was essential that whoever controlled the city of New Orleans not interfere with American shipping. Prior to ceding the territory back to France, Spain had revoked an earlier agreement with America that had granted duty-free transshipment of goods through New Orleans and access to temporary storage facilities in that city.

Therefore, it was clear that American ownership of New Orleans would be preferable to dependence on the French, or whoever else might come to control New Orleans. With this in mind, Jefferson instructed Robert Livingston, the U.S. minister in Paris, to negotiate the purchase of New Orleans from France. Thus was set in motion a negotiating process that would produce surprising results—and change the geography of the United States forever.

When Livingston began his negotiations, the French did not seem very eager to conclude an agreement. The talks dragged on for several months with seemingly little progress. Then the atmosphere changed. Livingston had hinted that America might be interested in establishing closer ties with Britain. Napoleon, sensing that renewed war with Britain was imminent, realized that he could not afford to risk having America become Britain's ally. In addition, he needed funds to finance the war.

Suddenly, the French made an amazing proposal to Livingston, who by this time had been joined in the negotiations by James Monroe. Not only would they sell New Orleans, but they would be willing to sell the entire Louisiana Territory to America! This was more than the Americans could ever have hoped for; they jumped at the chance to acquire the huge territory in a purchase that would prove to be the most incredible land bargain in U.S. history.

The Louisiana Purchase was signed on May 2, 1803. For a payment of $15,000,000, America bought 828,000 square miles, doubling the size of the country. The Louisiana Territory, which reached from the Mississippi River westward to the Rocky Mountains, and north to the border of British Canada, included what are now the states of Louisiana, Missouri, Arkansas, Iowa, North Dakota, South Dakota, Nebraska, and Oklahoma, and included most of the land in Minnesota, Kansas, Colorado, Wyoming, and Montana. On October 20, 1803, Congress ratified the Louisiana Purchase, and on December 20, France officially turned over the Louisiana Territory to the United States.

**CELEBRATION OF THE LOUISIANA PURCHASE**

Since not very much was known about the Louisiana Territory at that time, and even the borders were somewhat vague, Jefferson lost no time in drawing up plans to explore the vast expanse of lands west of the Mississippi. The area would soon become available for settlement, and Jefferson was eager to learn as much as possible about America's newest region, including its geography, geology, flora and fauna, as well as its Native American inhabitants and their customs.

Therefore to gather all of this information, Jefferson sent out an expedition headed by Captain Meriwether Lewis and Lieutenant William Clark to explore the territory. Their instructions were to find the source of the Missouri River, and then cross the mountains forming the western border of the territory and continue their explorations all the way to the Pacific Ocean. Jefferson hoped that they would discover the Northwest Passage, a river rumored to provide an overland route to the Pacific.

Lewis and Clark began their epic journey of discovery on May 14, 1804, at St. Louis, on the banks of the Mississippi. The forty members of the expedition traveled in three boats. Ten miles upriver from St. Louis, at the confluence of the Mississippi and Missouri Rivers, they started up the Missouri. By November they arrived in what is now North Dakota. There they spent the winter, among the friendly Mandan Sioux tribe.

*MERIWETHER LEWIS*

In the spring they set out walking westward across the plains, accompanied by a French-Canadian guide named Toussaint Charbonneau, his 17-year-old Shoshoni wife Sacagawea, and her infant son Pomp, whom she carried on her back. When they reached the Rocky Mountains, they entered Shoshoni country. Upon encountering a band of Shoshoni, Sacagawea, who served as the expedition's interpreter, suddenly began "to dance and show every mark of joy," as Clark noted in his diary. Sacagawea had recognized one of the Shoshoni as her brother Cameauhwait, whom she had not seen since childhood. Cameauhwait, a chief of the Shoshoni, provided guides and horses for the expedition.

The party crossed the Continental Divide and continued westward. When they reached the Clearwater River, they built canoes and traveled down the Clearwater to the Snake, and then to the Columbia, which they followed all the way to the river's mouth at the Pacific Ocean. It was now November 15, 1805. An ecstatic Clark wrote in his diary, "Ocean in view! O! the joy." After spending a difficult winter on the beach, the expedition traveled east, crossing the mountains once again, and eventually traveling downstream on the Missouri River. They arrived in St. Louis on September 23,1806, 28 months after their journey began.

Lewis and Clark had successfully carried out the first overland expedition to the Pacific Ocean and back. Lewis wrote to Jefferson, "In obedience to your orders we have penetrated the continent of North America to the Pacific Ocean." Amazingly, nobody had been killed on the journey, although one man had died of appendicitis. Lewis and Clark sent Jefferson their maps and their diaries filled with a treasure trove of knowledge about the lands they had explored, and they informed him that the Northwest Passage was just a myth. Jefferson rewarded Lewis and Clark with 1,600 acres of land, and the other expedition members with 320 acres each.

Shortly after Lewis and Clark had begun their journey of exploration, two of the country's most well-known political figures brought their long-standing feud to a tragic conclusion. On July 11, 1804 in Weehawken, New Jersey, Vice-President Aaron Burr fought a duel with his arch enemy, Alexander Hamilton. Rivalry and enmity between the two went back a long time. They had often clashed when both were officers in the Continental Army. Then they had been rivals in the New York law courts. Later the two had fought each other when

***DUEL BETWEEN AARON BURR AND ALEXANDER HAMILTON***

Hamilton was Secretary of the Treasury and Burr was a senator from New York. Finally, after helping deny Burr the chance to become president in 1800, Hamilton in 1804 was again instrumental in preventing Burr from gaining a political office—this time the governorship of New York State.

Several weeks after losing the election, Burr was shown an old newspaper, in which there was a letter containing these sentences: "General Hamilton and Judge Kent have declared, in substance, that they looked upon Mr. Burr to be a dangerous man, and one who ought not to be trusted with the reins of government. . . . I could detail to you a still more despicable opinion which General Hamilton has expressed of Mr. Burr." This was the final straw. Burr felt compelled to challenge Hamilton to a duel. Hamilton felt compelled to accept the challenge. And so the long-standing rivalry came to an end as Burr fatally wounded his enemy, who died the next day, after several hours of agonizing pain.

*JAMES WILKINSON*

Burr was shocked at the angry reaction of the public to the duel. After all, duels were still an acceptable way of settling differences at that time. Other public figures, such as New York Mayor DeWitt Clinton and Judge Brockholst Livingston had participated in duels without such an outcry. Yet now the state of New Jersey wanted to try Burr on a charge of murder! Burr fled to the South, spending the next several months in hiding in South Carolina, Georgia, and Spanish Florida. The furor eventually died down, and Burr returned to Washington to his post as vice president and presiding officer of the Senate.

Burr now knew that he had no chance of ever being elected president, and that in a few months he would no longer be vice president. Indeed, when Jefferson was reelected on December 5, 1804, George Clinton became vice president. So the ever ambitious Burr began scheming with a friend, Major General James Wilkinson, then governor of the Louisiana Territory, to establish a revolutionary party and create an empire in the southwest. Burr attracted hundreds of followers to his cause with his promises of fabulous fortunes to be made, and raised a considerable amount of money.

However, when Burr began speaking about possibly invading Spanish Florida, starting a revolution in Mexico, or even persuading the western states to secede and elect him president, Wilkinson became alarmed. Considering Burr to be delusional and doomed to fail, Wilkinson reported Burr's conspiracy to Jefferson.

Burr was arrested and tried for treason, with plotting war against the United States, and planning to attack New Orleans. However, at his trial Burr was acquitted by Chief Justice John Marshall on a constitutional technicality. Marshall ruled that Burr was not "actually or constructively present" during an overt act of treason. Burr would spend the rest of his life in relative obscurity, residing in Europe for several years before returning to New York.

A year after the signing of the Louisiana Purchase, Jefferson was reelected in a landslide vote. When he began his second term in 1805, the British and French were still at war, and tensions were growing between America and the two warring nations. Both nations were once again seizing American merchant vessels with impunity, and confiscating millions of dollars worth of American goods in the process. In addition, the British were still kidnapping American crews, forcing them to serve on British warships. Some 10,000 Americans were to suffer this fate. Americans were outraged and many were eager to go to war, but Jefferson hoped to avoid conflict.

At his first presidential inauguration in 1801, Jefferson had announced a foreign policy of "peace, commerce, and honest friendship with all nations—entangling alliances with none." In 1805, Jefferson still hoped to keep America out of war and maintain a status of neutrality. However, something had to be done to protest British and French actions. Jefferson and Secretary of State James Madison believed that commerce could be used as a means of "peaceful coercion." So with that strategy in mind, Congress in 1806 passed a Non-Importation Act, prohibiting the importation of British goods. Unfortunately this did nothing to deter the British.

After the British ship *H.M.S. Leopard* opened fire on the *U.S.S. Chesapeake* in June 1807, killing three Americans, Jefferson took a stronger measure, signing the Embargo Act on December 22. The Embargo Act prohibited the export of American goods to any foreign ports, thus depriving Britain and France of access to American goods, or so Jefferson and Madison hoped. Unfortunately, the British and French were able to obtain all the goods they needed from American smugglers. Worse, the trade embargo hurt America more than Britain or France, because of the loss of markets for America's exports.

The embargo policy provoked much bitterness among Americans, especially New England merchants, who saw it as a major infringement of their rights. Jefferson bore the brunt of their resentment, suffering a loss in popularity. Some New England Federalists were so angry about the embargo that they threatened to have their states secede from the Union. So on March 1, 1809, just three days before leaving office, Jefferson signed the Non-Intercourse Act, which repealed the Embargo Act and allowed American trade to resume with all other nations except Britain and France.

# ONE NATION—TWO ECONOMIES

The country's first strong political leaders—George Washington and Thomas Jefferson—did their best to make sure the young nation of 13 states became unified as a republic. However, their job was made more difficult because of conflicting economic interests, particularly the growing differences between the industrial North and the agricultural South.

Most Americans at the time were part of an agrarian economy consisting mainly of small farmers and settlers as well as wealthy Southern planters. Their interests were best represented by the Republicans. Jefferson, the leading Republican spokesman, would have been happy to live in an America consisting solely of farmers, but as president he also had to consider the interests of the rising merchant

*SAMUEL SLATER'S MILL*

class of the northeastern towns and cities.

Jefferson believed that agriculture was the basic producer of wealth, and that the government's most important task was to find markets for America's goods. Hamilton, on the other hand, thought the American government should encourage economic development through manufacturing along the lines of the Industrial Revolution taking place in Britain. Hamilton and the Federalists sought to promote the interests of the wealthy northern businessmen—merchants, bankers, and other assorted entrepreneurs and financiers. They favored the growth of new industry, such as the textile industry that had begun to develop in New England.

For example, in 1793, Samuel Slater, with the financial backing of Moses Brown, had started America's first cotton spinning mill in Pawtucket, Rhode Island. In 1814, in Waltham, Massachusetts, Francis Cabot Lowell would establish the first American mill that carded, spun thread, and wove cloth under one roof.

*CORNELIUS VANDERBILT*

While the textile industry would bring prosperity to many New England towns, other businesses such as shipbuilding brought prosperity to coastal towns such as Salem, Massachusetts, where wealthy ship owners grew even richer through overseas trade. Meanwhile, New York, with its stock exchange, busy port, and warehouses, was rapidly becoming the nation's main center of commerce. Taking advantage of this situation, an enterprising young New Yorker by the name of Cornelius Vanderbilt began operating a ferry service between Staten Island and Manhattan. In so doing, he had embarked on the first crucial step in building what would become one of the 19th century's largest and most successful family businesses.

Because Jefferson saw agricultural development in America as a vital economic necessity, one of his goals was to make as much land as possible available to settlers who would farm it. Prior to the Revolutionary War, Britain had prohibited white settlement of lands west of the Appalachians, in places such as the Ohio Valley. The thriving fur trade that had developed there between white merchants and Native Americans would have been threatened by such settlement. Of course, this trade was much more beneficial to the white merchants than to the Native Americans; unfortunately, traders often gave Native Americans whiskey in exchange for their furs. So while many Indian tribes suffered the devastating effects of alcoholism, fur traders such as John Jacob Astor grew very wealthy during this period.

***John Jacob Astor***

By 1801, Jefferson began to realize the desirability of removing Native Americans from their land in order to open up the area to white farmers. He then saw the Louisiana Purchase as an opportunity to resettle Native Americans in the new Louisiana Territory. And in the Louisiana Territory Act of 1804, the federal government openly declared for the first time its intention of moving Native Americans living east of the Mississippi River to the west. Sadly, the movement of Native Americans would not end here, as there would be more forced migrations to come.

As more land opened up for settlement, farm production increased. However, transporting produce to market, an essential part of the agricultural economy, was problematical in many instances. One industrial innovation of the period that would help farmers was the steamboat. At the time, transportation on land was difficult, slow, and expensive because there were few good roads. Farmers depended on access to river transport.

Shipping products by boat became more expedient after 1807, the year Robert Fulton's steamboat *Clermont* made its successful maiden voyage up the Hudson River from New York to Albany. Although Fulton relied upon the inventions of others in building his boat, he was the first to demonstrate that transporting passengers and goods by steamboat was not only possible, but practical. Within a few years, the steamboat, originally referred to by a skeptical public as "Fulton's Folly," would be providing regular service as far west as the Mississippi.

*FULTON'S FIRST STEAMSHIP*

Another technological innovation of the period would benefit the Southern plantation, a large farming enterprise that depended on the labor of enslaved African Americans to grow crops such as tobacco, rice, and cotton. In 1793 Eli Whitney invented the cotton gin, a device that made it possible to mechanize the arduous task of removing cotton seeds from the fiber. Before 1793, it was impractical to grow cotton except along the Georgia and South Carolina coasts, where a certain type of cotton grew. After the introduction of the cotton gin, cotton spread throughout the South, and came to be referred to as "King Cotton."

*ROBERT FULTON*

One unfortunate consequence of the cotton gin would be the increased demand for slave labor. Before the sudden increase in cotton production, the evil institution of slavery was becoming somewhat tenuous. Tobacco production was declining, and there was a growing revulsion by many Americans against

*THE COTTON GIN*

the abuses of the slave trade. Even in the South, the prospect of gradual emancipation was becoming a real possibility. South Carolina had actually abolished the slave trade in 1787. However, almost overnight cotton had brought about a reversal, and South Carolina reinstated slavery in 1803. By 1810, one-third of the total population of the South consisted of slaves.

Although most of the enslaved Africans who had been brought to America were sold to planters in Georgia and South Carolina, before the Revolutionary War there were slaves in all of the thirteen original colonies, including those in the North. Indeed, leading merchants in New England, especially Rhode Island, were deeply involved in the slave trade, purchasing people in Africa, transporting them across the Atlantic in horrid conditions aboard crowded slave ships, and selling them in the colonies.

Before the Revolutionary War, many of the founding fathers, who were so devoted to the concept of freedom, were themselves slaveholders. The farm work at George Washington's Mount Vernon home was done by enslaved African Americans, as was the case at Thomas Jefferson's beautiful Monticello estate. However, during the war, Virginia stopped importing slaves, and after the war, Virginia planter George Mason led a movement against the slave trade. By 1807, all states except Georgia and South Carolina had banned the slave trade. And on March 2, 1807, at President Jefferson's direction, Congress banned the importation of slaves into the United States effective January 1, 1808.

Unfortunately an illegal slave trade continued, as well as an internal slave trade between the states. Over the next 50 years, the issue would grow increasingly controversial, with cries for slavery's abolition, coming mainly from the northern states, against the determination of southern states to exercise "states' rights" and continue an institution that kept their economy strong. Eventually, the inability of the North and the South to come to an accommodation on this volatile issue would lead to the catastrophe of the Civil War.

***SLAVES PICKING COTTON IN GEORGIA***

# JAMES MADISON AND THE ROAD TO WAR

When Republican James Madison, the "Father of the Constitution," was inaugurated as president on March 4, 1809, war was still raging between Britain and France. Although both nations wanted access to America's products, each insisted that the United States trade exclusively with them. Both sides had issued decrees against neutral shipping—in other words, Britain was determined to prevent American products from reaching France, and France was determined to stop American trade with Britain. As did the presidents who preceded him, Madison sought to maintain American neutrality. During the Jefferson administration, Madison, as secretary of state, had been instrumental in establishing and enforcing the Embargo Act and then the Non-Intercourse Act, which kept in place an embargo against trade with Britain and France.

Now, hoping to normalize trade relations with Britain and France, Madison naively trusted first Britain and then France when those countries promised to rescind their decrees against neutral trade. Madison resumed American trade with Britain on April 29, 1809, only to have to reinstate the Non-Intercourse Act on August 9, when he learned that Britain had annulled the agreement that British and American offi-

*James Madison*

cials had reached in April. A similar course of failed diplomacy occurred between America and France.

For the next two years, Britain and France toyed with America regarding the status of trade relations, as if the new nation were a helpless pawn caught between both powers. One agreement after another was signed and then rescinded, because neither Britain nor France was ever serious about allowing America to engage in neutral shipping. Both sides continued to seize American ships, and Britain, adding insult to injury, continued to impress American sailors into service on British warships.

As expected, American anger was steadily growing during this time. Fearing that war might ultimately be unavoidable, on November 5, 1811, Madison asked Congress for increased defense spending in preparation for possible conflict against Britain. In response, Congress authorized major increases in military enlistments and the call-up of 100,000 militia, and approved additional funds for the navy.

Americans had another reason to be angry at the British. After the Revolutionary War, American settlers began pouring into lands occupied by Native Americans. Treaties were often imposed on the Native American tribes by the American government, but these were usually ignored by both white settlers and Native Americans. Until 1796, Britain retained control of various forts in upstate New York and in the Northwest Territories. Native Americans, with the help of the British, had organized confederacies during the 1790s in the Northwest Territories, and

*TENSKWATAWA*

had engaged in warfare to resist the advance of white settlement.

At the time, the American government's policy was to encourage assimilation of Native Americans into the white culture. Some tribes, such as the Cherokee in the South, accepted this policy, building cabins and learning farming techniques from the white settlers. Other Native Americans in the South, such as the Creek, and those in the Northwest, were determined to resist white encroachment on their land and their culture.

In 1805, in the Indiana Territory, a Shawnee religious leader known as Tenskwatawa, "the Prophet," and his brother, Chief Tecumseh, began to organize local tribes into the Shawnee Confederacy. During the next few years, government treaties, negotiated by William Henry Harrison, Governor of the Indiana Territory, took away huge tracts of Shawnee land. Tecumseh and his brother continued to organize for warfare, promising the Indians that the British would help them win back their lands.

On November 6, 1811, while Tecumseh was attempting to organize Indians in the South, a force of one thousand U.S. troops under Governor Harrison's command were preparing to attack the headquarters of the Shawnee Confederacy at the headwaters of the Tippecanoe River. Shawnee braves, led by Tenskwatawa, staged a surprise attack on Harrison's soldiers. The attack failed, however, and the surviving Shawnee fled, leaving behind their British arms. This evidence of British involvement would increase the clamor for war against Britain. Meanwhile, Tecumseh and his followers crossed into Canada, where they would join British forces in the coming war.

***TECUMSEH***

Opinion in Congress differed as to who was America's worst enemy. The Federalists saw France as the enemy, and they opposed a war against Britain. However, the Republican "War Hawks," led by Congressional leaders such as Henry Clay of Kentucky and John C. Calhoun of South Carolina, demanded that the United States stand up to British intimidation—hostile acts at sea and stirring up an Indian war from bases in Canada—and once and for all demon-

***THE BATTLE OF TIPPECANOE***

strate America's ability and willingness to defend its rights. According to the War Hawks, America would easily conquer all of Canada, as well as Mexico and Florida, and add these territories to the United States. After the Battle of Tippecanoe, they took up the cry "On to Canada!"

Finally giving in to the inevitable, Madison reached an agreement with the War Hawks; he promised to call for war if they would back him for another term as president in the election in 1812. On June 1, 1812, Madison sent a war message to Congress, citing British impressment of American sailors, violations of American neutral trade, and incitement of Indian warfare on the western frontier as the causes for engaging in hostilities with Great Britain. On June 4, the House of Representatives approved a declaration of war against Britain; on June 17, the Senate did the same, and Madison signed the declaration the following day. The War Hawks kept their part of the bargain, too, and on March 4, 1813, Madison would be inaugurated for a second term.

While the War Hawks believed that America would be fighting a second war for independence, New England Federalists believed the war would not be in their interests. On July 2, acting governor John Cotton Smith of Connecticut refused the federal government's request for militia. And on August 5, Massachusetts Governor Caleb Strong did the same. As events unfolded, Federalist opposition to the war would eventually grow so strong that in December, 1814, shortly before the war ended, Federalists from Massachusetts, Rhode Island, and Connecticut would meet at Hartford to discuss secession from the United States and the signing of a separate peace treaty with Great Britain.

# THE WAR OF 1812: "ON TO CANADA!"

America's strategy to win the war was to attack the British in the north in the belief that while Britain was a mighty sea power, the British were vulnerable in Canada. So the United States decided to risk a land war, hoping for a quick victory and end to the conflict. This seemed like a brilliant strategy to the War Hawks, who, while shouting "On to Canada," envisioned the campaign as not much more than a military parade through Canada. Indeed, Thomas Jefferson had said, "The acquisition of Canada this year as far as the neighborhood of Quebec, will be a mere matter of marching."

Unfortunately, the U.S. army was not prepared to successfully carry out such a strategy. The American high command—President Madison and General Henry Dearborn—would prove to be inept at effective military planning. There were few experienced officers to lead the army, except for the aging veterans of the Revolutionary War. In addition, because Republicans were generally opposed to levying taxes on Americans, military supplies were in short supply because of a lack of funding. The army itself, even with a rapid military build-up, consisted of fewer than 10,000 soldiers, many of them poorly trained, due to the Republicans' fear of a large standing army.

Great Britain's strategy was to beat back any American threat to

***Henry Dearborn***

Canada, while relying on its navy, the most powerful in the world, to blockade America's coast, crush the American navy, and finally invade the United States. As often happens in war, things did not go quite according to plan for both sides in this conflict.

The Americans got off to a bad start at the outset when the U.S. post on Michilimackinac Island in Michigan Territory surrendered to a force of British soldiers and their Indian allies on July 17, 1812. The following month, on August 15, the Shawnee attacked the American garrison at Fort Dearborn, Illinois (present-day Chicago), killing 85 soldiers and many of their dependents as they attempted to flee. The very next day, British troops under the command of General Isaac Brock and Shawnee led by Tecumseh were preparing to attack the American troops at Detroit. A timid General William Hull, receiving a false report that his troops were outnumbered, and fearing that everyone would be massacred by the enemy, surrendered Detroit without firing a shot.

When word of these early military disasters reached Washington, the War Hawks suddenly realized what the American forces were up against. Perhaps Canada would never fall into American hands. Forced to change their tune, they now focused their attention on successful naval encounters off the East Coast, crying "Free Trade and Seamen's Rights!" instead of the slogan "On to Canada." Fortunately for American morale, at about the same time as the military fiasco was occurring along the Canadian border, the U.S. Navy, with fewer than twenty ships, was

*WILLIAM HULL*

*THE* CONSTITUTION *DEFEATS THE* GUERRIERE

performing brilliantly against British ships in the Atlantic.

During the month of July 1812, the USS *Constitution*, a 44-gun frigate with copper-sheathed hulls, led a squadron of British warships on a merry chase through the waters off New England. The faster American ship easily slipped away from the pursuing British. Then, a month later, on August 19, the *Constitution*, commanded by Commodore Isaac Hull, engaged in a battle with the *Guerriere*, one of Britain's finest warships, off the coast of Nova Scotia. As the British cannonballs glanced harmlessly off the thick, reinforced hull of the *Constitution* (giving rise to the nickname "Old Ironsides"), the American frigate moved in close, firing broadsides that ripped the masts off the *Guerriere*, killing and wounding many of the crew. As the British frigate sank, the *Constitution* sailed back to Boston with 250 British prisoners aboard.

During the next six months, the Americans would win a series of stunning naval victories in the Atlantic. The USS *United States*, commanded by Captain Stephen Decatur, captured the British frigate *Macedonian*. The USS *Essex* captured the *Alert*. The USS *Constitution*, this time commanded by Commodore William Bainbridge, destroyed the British frigate *Java*. And the USS *Hornet* captured the *Peacock*.

Meanwhile, back along the Canadian border, the Americans were not having much luck. It eventually became clear that the planned invasion of Canada had no chance of success. On more than one occasion, the day would be lost for the Americans when some or all of the U.S. troops refused to fight. On October 13, 1812, General Stephen Van Rensselaer was wounded in the Battle of Queenston, fighting alongside the New York militia under his command. The Americans might have won this engagement, but some of the militia waiting on the New York side of the Niagara River and hearing the screams of the wounded, refused to cross over and join the battle against the British troops. The Americans again displayed a reluctance to fight at Stony Creek, Beaver Dams, and Chrysler's Farm.

On November 19, 1812, General Henry Dearborn had to abandon his plans to attack Montreal when his militia forces refused to cross into Canada. Then, on April 27, 1813, the Americans suffered another disaster. American forces under the command of Generals Dearborn and Zebulon Pike captured the town of York (present day Toronto). They had held the town for only a brief period and had begun burning public buildings when there was a sudden huge explosion. A powder magazine had blown up, killing Pike and 320 American troops.

It appeared as if nothing would ever go right for the Americans along the Canadian border. Then on September 10, 1813, Commodore Oliver Hazard Perry scored a major victory over a British fleet in a sea battle at the western end of Lake Erie near Put-in-Bay. Perry and his men fought bravely, no doubt inspired by a banner on Perry's ship which bore the words, "Don't give up the ship," reportedly the dying words of Captain James Lawrence of the USS

***AMERICAN FORCES ATTACK TORONTO***

***PERRY AT THE BATTLE OF LAKE ERIE***

*Chesapeake*, which had been sunk earlier that year. When Perry's ship had been blasted to pieces and most of his men killed or wounded, Perry and a few survivors rowed to another ship in his fleet and kept on fighting. After his victory, Perry wrote, "We have met the enemy, and they are ours."

The defeated British were forced out of Detroit, and America regained control of the Michigan Territory. Having destroyed the British fleet, Perry was now able to ferry 4,000 troops, under the command of General William Henry Harrison, to Ontario on the Canadian side of the lake. On October 5, Harrison and his soldiers reached Moravian Town, where they fought and defeated a combined force of British and Shawnee at the Battle of the Thames. During the battle, Chief Tecumseh was killed, thus putting an end to any further Indian resistance to white settlement in the Northwest. The Creeks in the South, however, whom Tecumseh had persuaded to join the war, were determined to fight on.

The Americans would win several more skirmishes against the British along the northern border, thereby turning what had been a losing campaign into a stalemate. While the American forces would never be able to successfully invade and take over Canada, at least they would prevent the British from penetrating most of the northern lands of the United States.

On July 5, 1814, U.S. Generals Jacob Brown and Winfield Scott led their forces across the Niagara River into Canada and defeated the British in the Battle of Chippewa. Then, on July 25, Brown and his men waged a hard-fought battle against the British at Lundy's Lane, Canada, near Niagara Falls. Throughout the encounter, both sides were firing at each other at close range, and the situation was so confusing that it was not clear who had the upper hand. By the time each side withdrew, both were claiming victory. Later that year, on September 11, Captain Thomas Macdonough led an American squadron to a decisive victory over the British fleet on Lake Champlain near Plattsburgh, New York. British General Sir George Prevost was now forced to abandon his plans for invading the United States from the north.

***THE DEATH OF TECUMSEH AT THE BATTLE OF THE THAMES***

# *THE WAR OF 1812: THE BATTLE OF THE COAST*

The British, at first caught off guard by the superior ships and seamanship of the Americans, were determined not to allow any nation to triumph over the might British navy. By December 12, 1812, the British navy had begun blockading the Delaware and Chesapeake Bays. On March 30, 1813, they extended their blockade of the East Coast from Long Island, New York, all the way to New Orleans, Louisiana.

A year later, on April 25, 1814, the British had further extended their blockade to New England. By this time, Britain had finally defeated Napoleon and France, thus freeing up additional forces for service in Canada and the United States. The British now

***British troops plundered and burned American cities***

***Sir George Cockburn***

*THE BRITISH BURNING OF WASHINGTON, D.C.*

deployed so many naval vessels along the Atlantic coast that U.S. ships would no longer be able to venture out to sea.

On August 8, 1814, peace negotiations between Great Britain and America began in Ghent, Belgium. Both sides had begun to realize that because the course of the war, up to this point, had been rather inconclusive, sooner or later it would be in the interests of both parties to conclude a peace agreement. However, that moment hadn't occurred yet, so while both sides began talking, the war continued.

The British were now in a position to carry out raids on towns up and down the East Coast, and they proceeded to do so. In New England, the British bombarded Stonington, Connecticut, destroying half the town. They also attacked Cape Cod in Massachusetts. And a British force from Canada invaded Maine, occupying the portion of the state east of the Penobscott River. Shipbuilders in the town of Bangor were forced to turn over their new ships to the British as soon as work on them was completed. Farther south, the British attacked Havre de Grace, Maryland, and Hampton, Virginia. In most places, the British plundered the towns, sometimes burning buildings and occasionally even killing citizens.

Unfortunately, because most of the American army and militia units were deployed along the northern border, many coastal towns were relatively defenseless. One city that was in imminent danger was Washington, D.C., the nation's new capital. Citizens of that city regarded the arrival of a large British fleet in Chesapeake Bay as an ominous sign. Women, children, and old men packed up and evacuated the city.

All able-bodied men assembled at nearby Bladensburg, Maryland, to organize a defense with a group of local militiamen. The several thousand Americans, whose armaments included cannons, waited there for the British. President Madison left the White House to join the defenders in Maryland, while his wife Dolley stayed behind to pack up important items, including the Gilbert Stuart portrait of George Washington, some official papers, and her parrot.

On August 24, the British forces under the command of General Robert Ross and Admiral Sir George Cockburn, came ashore about 40 miles from Washington, D.C. When the American defenders saw the British marching toward the city, they panicked. After a few exchanges of fire, the Americans fled, Madison among them. By evening, the British troops, encountering no further resistance, had entered Washington. Dolley Madison had managed to escape just in time as the British troops were entering the city. Almost immediately, the British set to work destroying Washington's most important buildings. They intended to retaliate for the American burning of York (Toronto) the year before. After setting fire to the Capitol, they headed for the White House. Admiral Cockburn went inside and scooped up a couple of souvenirs for himself—a cocked hat belonging to Madison, and the cushion from Dolley's favorite chair. When the British admiral came back outside and mounted his white horse, the White House was set ablaze. Soon other public buildings were also put to the torch.

***DOLLEY MADISON***

The next morning, while the British considered their next move, one of their men accidentally dropped a torch into a well containing barrels of gunpowder. In the ensuing explosion, several soldiers were killed. Then, a very strange thing happened—an event that probably saved the city of Washington from being totally reduced to rubble. A sudden, violent storm swept through the city. In the midst of the storm, a British soldier thought he saw a large American army in the distance approaching the city. The British commander ordered his troops to retreat, and they withdrew from Washington, never to return. Soon the Americans who had fled the city, including President Madison and his wife, began drifting back. They were greeted with the depressing sight of scorched and blackened government buildings.

***Francis Scott Key***

The burning of Washington was an absolute low point of the war for Americans and certainly the conflict's most humiliating episode. It might have had a long-lasting negative effect on the young nation's morale, if not for the fact that three weeks later, one of America's proudest moments of the war took place not far from Washington. On September 13, the British attempted to capture the city of Baltimore, Maryland. This time the Americans, who were outraged at the burning of their nation's capital, were determined to resist.

About 10,000 Americans hastily prepared to defend Baltimore, as the British attacked by land and by sea. At the outset, the British suffered a major blow. The battle had barely begun when British General Ross, riding at the head of his troops, was shot and killed by two young Americans. The British troops pulled back in disarray, to await the entry of the British warships into the Patapsco River. First, however, the ships had to get past Fort McHenry, the gateway to Baltimore.

The bombardment of little Fort McHenry began on the morning of September 13. The British guns, which had a much greater reach than those of the Americans, fired at the fort from a safe distance. The Americans could do nothing about it. However, whenever the British ships tried to get close to the fort, the American cannons roared to life, and the British, sustaining serious losses, had to retreat. The bombardment would continue without letup for 25 hours, as rockets and bombs rained

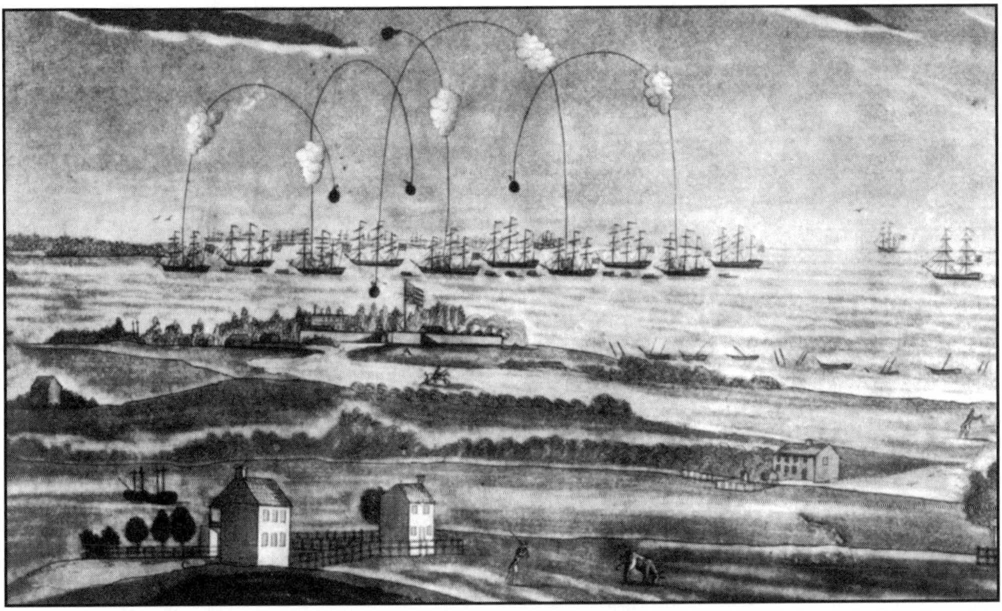

***BOMBING OF FORT MCHENRY***

down mercilessly on the 1,000 Americans bravely defending the fort.

Watching the battle throughout the long night from one of the British ships was Francis Scott Key, a Washington lawyer being held temporary prisoner aboard the ship. A week earlier, Key had sailed out to the ship seeking the release of a friend, another American being held prisoner.

Hour after hour, Key watched as the sky above Fort McHenry was lit up by the red glow of exploding rockets. When dawn finally came, Key was astonished to see that the American flag was still flying above the fort. Key felt so proud of the Americans' bravery that he was inspired to write down his patriotic feelings. His words in homage to "The Star-Spangled Banner" would eventually become famous as the lyrics of America's national anthem. Ironically, the words were set to a British tune, "To Anacreon in Heaven."

On September 14, Admiral Cockburn, realized that his forces would not be able to silence the cannons of Fort McHenry, and that his warships would not gain access to Baltimore. Therefore, he gave the order to stop the bombardment. Before the British ships sailed away in defeat, Key and his friend were released.

Although American self-esteem had been restored by the defense of Baltimore, the inconclusive nature of the war was becoming even more apparent to both sides in the conflict. There no longer seemed to be much point in prolonging the war. The time had now come for serious negotiations between the Americans and British at Ghent.

# THE WAR OF 1812: THE BATTLE OF NEW ORLEANS

Included among the five-man negotiating team in Ghent, Belgium, were Henry Clay, John Quincy Adams, and Albert Gallatin, a former Secretary of the Treasury. When the Americans first met with their British counterparts in August, 1814, they found the terms offered by the British totally unacceptable. The British at the time still assumed that they were negotiating from a position of strength. In their eyes, the Americans most likely feared a British invasion and would perhaps agree to Britain's terms. The Americans, however, rejected the British conditions for peace.

*THE TREATY OF GHENT*

By October, the negotiators on both sides had learned of the American defeat of the British fleet on Lake Champlain. They now knew that Britain would be unable to invade the United States from the north. They had also learned of the British fleet's failure to capture Baltimore, or any other major American city, even though they had managed to humiliate the Americans by burning Washington, D.C. Finally, when the British government tried to persuade their greatest military leader, the Duke of Wellington, to take charge of British forces in North America, he refused, saying that Britain was not entitled to any territorial claims against the United States. Therefore, both sides were motivated to engage in serious negotiations.

On December 24, 1814, the United States and Britain signed a peace treaty at Ghent. The terms of the treaty specified that there would be no territorial changes, except that all occupied territory, such as the eastern part of Maine, would be returned. Settlement of all other unresolved issues, such as matters pertaining to free trade and the rights of seamen, would be postponed until a later date. Any disputes over boundary lines would also be dealt with later by boards of commissioners. As if to emphasize the fact that serious issues had yet to be resolved, the treaty made no mention of the causes of the war. In any event, hostilities between America and Britain were to cease as soon as the treaty was ratified by both sides.

*The Duke of Wellington*

As far as both nations were concerned, for all practical purposes the war was over with the signing of the treaty, and the combatants could now lay down their arms. Of course, in 1814, instant communications did not yet exist, and word from Europe to America traveled slowly. So, while a peace treaty had been signed, the war continued because people in America were unaware of the agreement. Indeed, a major battle was yet to occur at New Orleans, a battle that need never have been fought.

During the final weeks of the treaty negotiations, the British had ordered an attack on New Orleans, expecting to achieve a decisive victory and put additional pressure on the Americans to agree to their terms. Andrew Jackson, who was commanding an army in the vicinity, learned of the British plans at the last minute. In his hasty preparations for the defense of New Orleans, he enlisted the help of various groups to supplement his military force. Joining Jackson's regular army troops and militia from Kentucky, Tennessee, and Louisiana, were free

*ANDREW JACKSON AT THE BATTLE OF NEW ORLEANS*

African American volunteers, Choctaw Indians, and the pirate Jean Laffite and his men. Jackson's forces began digging defensive trenches in the swamps along the Mississippi River, a few miles east of the city.

Nicknamed "Old Hickory" by his soldiers, because it was the toughest thing they could think of, Jackson had led the Tennessee militia to a decisive victory over the Creek Indians earlier that year. In recognition, he was given the rank of major-general in the regular army and the command of the Seventh Military District, which included Tennessee, Louisiana, and the Mississippi Territory. The Creek nation had long resented the expansion of white settlement into their lands in Georgia and the Mississippi Territory (present-day Mississippi and Alabama), an expansion that had increased with the Louisiana Purchase. In 1811, Tecumseh had encouraged the Creeks to fight for their lands, promising that the British would help them against the Americans. When war broke out between America and Britain in 1812, the Creeks saw this as their opportunity to take back their lands.

On August 30, 1813, a force of about 1,000 Creeks attacked Fort Mims, north of Mobile in the Mississippi Territory. They inflicted a deadly blow, killing more than 250 soldiers and settlers. Only 15 settlers managed to escape the slaughter. In November of that year, several other battles between Creeks and whites took place, during which the

*THE BATTLE OF NEW ORLEANS*

***THE DEATH OF MAJOR GENERAL SIR EDWARD PAKENHAM***

Creeks lost numerous warriors. Then Jackson was given orders to put an end to the Creek uprising, once and for all. Accompanied by Davy Crockett and Sam Houston, he led a force of 2,000 militiamen and 200 friendly Cherokee through more than 100 miles of Alabama wilderness, attacking the Creek settlement at Horseshoe Bend on the Tallapoosa River on March 27, 1814. In the ensuing battle, 550 Creeks, more than half their number, were killed. Hundreds more were killed trying to escape.

The surviving Creeks now realized they would never be able to retake their lands. On August 9, 1814, Jackson presented them with a treaty they were forced to accept, no matter how harsh it may have been. The Treaty of Fort Jackson obliged the Creeks to give up any claims to nearly 23 million acres of land—approximately one-fifth of Georgia and three-fifths of present-day Alabama.

With the danger posed by the Creeks eliminated, Jackson now turned his attention to the threat from British forces. He marched his army down to Pensacola in Spanish Florida, and believing that the old Spanish town now belonged to the British, he attacked and captured it. Then Jackson learned that a fleet of British warships was waiting off Cuba, preparing to attack the mainland. Jackson assumed that the British would land at Mobile, so he led his forces there. However, he soon found out that the British were actually planning on land-ing on the Louisiana coast opposite New Orleans. Jackson rushed his army back to New Orleans, arriving there in nine days, and immediately set about preparing for the attack.

On the morning of January 8, 1815, two weeks after the signing of the Treaty of Ghent, the British launched their attack. Leading the British frontal assault was 37-year-old Major General Sir Edward Pakenham, brother-in-law of the Duke of Wellington. The 6,000 advancing British troops in their red coats marched in columns 60 abreast. Jackson's men, greatly outnumbered, waited in their trenches until the British came within firing range. Then the Americans let loose one round after another of artillery and rifle fire. The British soldiers went down, row by row, cut to pieces by the American guns. Before long, more than 2,000 British soldiers had either been killed or wounded. Among the dead were General Pakenham and two other British generals. The Battle of New Orleans, the bloodiest of the war, was over—and the Americans had won a stunning victory. Amazingly, there were only 21 American casualties!

News of the American victory at New Orleans spread throughout the country; it reached Washington on February 11, the same day word arrived of the signing of the Treaty of Ghent. The timing of this convergence was even more remarkable because on that same day, a delegation from Hartford, Connecticut had arrived in Washington to threaten secession of the New England states unless their demands were met. When these New Englanders heard the startling news, they beat a hasty retreat back home lest they appear ridiculous, or worse, be accused of treason.

Ironically, the Battle of New Orleans should never have been fought, and its casualties should never have been inflicted. However, unnecessary as it was, Americans had good reason to celebrate this decisive victory over the British. It served to lessen the painful memories of the many humiliations the United States had suffered during the previous three years of the war. This victory allowed many Americans to believe that the United States had actually won the war, and certainly helped diminish whatever frustrations Americans might have felt about the truly inconclusive outcome of the conflict.

President Madison was given credit for defending the new nation's honor. The United States emerged from what many considered to be its "second war of independence" as a nation finally in control of its own destiny. It had gained the respect of other nations, letting them know that it would no longer stand for violation of its neutral trading rights or the impressment of its sailors. In addition, now that the war was over, normal trade relations could resume between America and Britain—and from that point forward, the two nations would only be allies, never enemies, in future wars.

# Where to Go

This section is designed as your guide to parks, historic sites, museums, and interpretive centers in the United States and its territories, where you can go to see what life was like in the historical period covered by *Rise of a New Nation.*

At these sites, you can see where many of the events in the book actually took place, or view exhibits relating to the everyday lives of the people who lived and worked in America in the period from 1787 to 1815 and beyond.

**1. Horseshoe Bend National Military Park**
11288 Horseshoe Bend Road
Daviston, AL 36256
(205) 234-7111
www.nps.gov/hobe/

Horseshoe Bend in Alabama is the site of the final battle of the Creek War of 1813-1814. General Andrew Jackson's forces launched a devastating attack against the Creeks, who had built a large wooden barricade across a peninsula formed by the "horseshoe" shaped bend of the Tallapoosa River. Over 800 Creeks died defending their way of life, and the survivors were forced to give up most of their lands.

**2. Arkansas Post National Memorial**
Gillett, AR 72055
(501) 548-2207
www.gov.nps./arpo

Located six miles south of Gillett, Arkansas, on U.S. Route 165, and two miles east on State Route 169, the memorial comprises 389 acres on the banks of the Arkansas River in southeastern Arkansas. The Louisiana Territory, purchased in 1803, was officially handed over to the United States by France at a fort on the bluffs overlooking the Arkansas River in 1804. The fort was renamed Fort Madison, but after the U.S. garrison departed in 1812, it fell into ruin, and no trace of it remains because of the river's erosion of the bluffs.

**3. Eli Whitney Museum**
915 Whitney Avenue
Hamden, CT 06517
(203) 777-1833
www.eliwhitney.org

The museum features changing exhibitions concerning the history of manufacturing and the effect of technological innovations, such as Eli Whitney's cotton gin, on American society. Also on display are firearms related to the Whitney armory, and an 1816 barn.

*Assembly room where the Declaration of Independence and the Constitution were signed*

**4. Mystic Seaport**
75 Greenmanville Avenue
Mystic, CT 06355
(860) 572-0711
www.mysticseaport.org

This recreation of a historic early-19th-century New England maritime village features exhibits of items representing America's historic relationship with the sea. On display are historic sailing ships, as well as maritime art, artifacts, manuscripts, ships' plans, and maps and charts. There is also a working shipyard and boat-building shop.

**5. Thomas Jefferson Memorial**
National Capital Parks-Central
900 Ohio Drive, SW
Washington, DC 20242
(202) 426-6841

The Thomas Jefferson Memorial, situated on 18 acres adjacent to the Potomac River in Washington, D.C., is a circular marble structure crowned by a low dome and encircled by a colonnade of classical Ionic columns. Inside is a 19-foot-high bronze statue of President Jefferson by sculptor Rudolph Evans. The memorial's design reflects Jefferson's architectural designs for his Virginia home, Monticello.

**6. National Archives**
700 Pennsylvania Avenue
Washington, DC 20408
(202) 501-5500
www.nara.gov

The National Archives are the nation's historical archives, which include a huge photo collection and numerous research materials. On display here are the original Declaration of Independence, the Constitution, and the Bill of Rights.

**7. The Smithsonian Institution**
1000 Jefferson Drive, S.W.
Room 370 MRC 033
Washington, DC 20560
(202) 357-2700
www.si.edu

The Smithsonian Institution includes numerous museums, art galleries, and research facilities. One of these, the National Museum of American History, exhibits the scientific, cultural, technological, and political development of the United States.

**8. Washington Monument**
National Capital Parks-Central
900 Ohio Drive, SW
Washington, DC 20242
(202) 426-6841

Situated on 106 acres midway between the U.S. Capitol and the Lincoln Memorial in Washington, D.C., the Washington Monument is a 555-foot-tall marble obelisk dedicated to the memory and accomplishments of George Washington, who served as commander-in-chief of American forces in the Revolutionary War, presiding officer of the Constitutional Convention in 1787 that drafted the U.S. Constitution, and the first president of the United States, from 1789 to 1797.

**9. The White House**
1600 Pennsylvania Avenue, N.W.
Washington, DC 20500
(202) 456-2550

The White House, situated on 18 acres between Lafayette Square and the Mall, at 1600 Pennsylvania Avenue, has been the home of all U.S. presidents since George Washington. It was designed by architect James Hoban and patterned after Irish Georgian-style country mansions. British troops set fire to the White House on August 24, 1814, during the War of 1812. Reconstruction was completed in 1817.

**10. Nez Perce National Historic Park**
Spalding, ID 83551
(208) 843-2261

The park comprises 2,109 acres in 38 scattered sites in Idaho, Washington, Oregon, and Montana. Canoe Camp and Long Camp are part of the Lewis and Clark National Historic Trail. Canoe Camp, 2.5 miles west of Orofino, Idaho, on U.S. Route 121, is an encampment site by the Clearwater River, where Lewis and Clark rested and built five canoes in the early autumn of 1805, before setting off toward the Pacific Ocean. Long Camp, just south of Kamiah, Idaho, on U.S. Route 12, is the site of an encampment where Lewis and Clark, in the spring of 1806, awaited the melting of the snow in the Bitterroot Range on their homeward journey.

**11. Fort Dearborn**
South end of Michigan Avenue Bridge
(Site marked by a plaque.)
Chicago, IL

In 1803 a blockhouse and stockade were built at this site at a narrow bend of the Chicago River because of Indian unrest. The fort was named for Henry Dearborn, a Revolutionary War hero. In 1812, soldiers and their dependents left the fort and were massacred by Indians just south of the fort along the shore of Lake Michigan.

**12. Native American Museum**
5170 East Poplar Street
Terre Haute, IN 47803
(812) 877-6007

Museum collections concentrate on Indiana history from prehistoric to modern times, with special emphasis on the history of the native tribes of the western Great Lakes, Wabash River Valley, and Ohio's Lower River Valley. Exhibits include a wigwam, longhouse, tools, and materials for cooking, clothing, basketry, weapons, and dolls.

**13. Tippecanoe Battlefield**
West Lafayette, IN
www.tcha.mus.in.us

This site is located near Interstate 65, just north of West Lafayette, Indiana. Take the exit for State Route 43 and follow signs to the battleground, where on November 6, 1811, General William Henry Harrison defeated the Shawnee led by Chief Tecumseh's brother "the Prophet." The site of the Battle of Tippecanoe is well preserved and includes an excellent museum.

**14. Vincennes**
Vincennes Chamber of Commerce
417 Busseron Street
Vincennes, IN 47591

The city of Vincennes, Indiana, founded as a French trading post in 1683, and renamed Fort Sackville by the British in 1763, was captured by George Rogers Clark during the Revolutionary War. From 1800 to 1813, the area was governed from the Indiana Territorial Capitol. Near the capitol building is a reconstruction of the newspaper office that held Indiana's first press. William Henry Harrison built Grouseland, which now exhibits family portraits and furnishings, while he was the territorial governor.

**15. Ashland, the Henry Clay Estate**
120 Sycamore Road
Lexington, KY 40502
(606) 266-8581
www.henryclay.org

This historic house (1811), situated on 18 acres of greenspace including a 1/2-acre garden, was the estate of Henry Clay. There is a collection of family furnishings, and guided tours are available.

**16. Cumberland Gap National Historic Park**
Middlesboro, KY 40965
(606) 248-2817
www.nps.gov/cuga

The park, consisting of 20,312 acres in Kentucky, Tennessee, and the western tip of Virginia, features the gap in the Appalachian Mountains that provided a route for white settlers heading west. In 1792, Kentucky became the 15th state, and by 1800, more than 300,000 people had poured through the Cumberland Gap.

**17. The Historic New Orleans Collection**
533 Royal Street
New Orleans, LA 70130
(504) 523-4662
www.hnoc.org

The History Museum and Research Center, housed in the Jean Francois Merieult House (1792) located in the French Quarter of New Orleans, includes books, manuscripts, paintings, drawings, prints, and maps pertaining to New Orleans history, including the Battle of New Orleans.

**18. Jean Lafitte National Historic Park and Preserve**
365 Canal Street, Suite 2400
New Orleans, LA 70130-1142
Chalmette Battlefield and National Cemetery
(504) 589-4430
www.nps.gov/jela/

The Chalmette Battlefield and National Cemetery, a part of the Jean Lafitte National Historic Park and Preserve, is located six miles southeast of New Orleans. It is the site of the Battle of New Orleans—the final battle of the War of 1812— in which American forces led by General Andrew Jackson won an overwhelmingly decisive victory over the British on January 8, 1815. The battle took place because neither side was aware that a peace treaty had been signed two weeks earlier.

**19. Maine State Museum**
State House Complex
Library/Archives Building
Augusta, ME 04330
(207) 289-2301
www.state.me.us/museum/

The museum features exhibits pertaining to Maine's natural resources, social history, and industrial heritage. The "Made in Maine" collection of 19th-century manufacturing equipment includes a textile factory and a water-powered woodworking mill.

**20. Penobscot Marine Museum**
Church Street
Searsport, ME
(207) 548-2529
www.penobscotmarinemuseum.org

The museum features marine paintings, models, and artifacts depicting the era of sail and trade, displayed in a group of buildings that includes several restored sea captain's homes, such as the Captain Merithew House, the old Town Hall, the Douglas and Margaret Carver Memorial Gallery, and the Phillips Memorial Library. The Town Hall contains ship models, shipbuilding tools, Asian trade objects, and a permanent exhibit relating to the large wooden ships built in Maine in the 19th century.

**21. Annapolis Historic District**
652 Main Street
Annapolis, MD 21401
www.annapolis.org

Annapolis was the nation's capital for a short time after the Revolution. Many restored buildings are open to the public, including the State House, the nation's oldest in continuous use. In addition, the U.S. Naval Academy (1845) houses a museum of U.S. naval history.

**22. Fort McHenry National Monument and Historic Shrine**
2400 East Fort Avenue
Baltimore, MD 21230
(410) 962-4290
www.nps.gov/fomc

Star-shaped Fort McHenry successfully defended the city of Baltimore from British attack during the War of 1812. The British bombarded the fort for 25 hours before they gave up. This American victory inspired Francis Scott Key to write to write the "Star-Spangled Banner." Visitors can tour the fort's batteries, barracks, and bastions.

**23. Fort Washington Park**
Indian Head Highway
Fort Washington, MD 20021

Fort Washington Park comprises 341 acres on the Maryland shore of the Potomac River, about six miles downriver from Washington, D.C. The first fort, built here in 1809 to protect the new nation's capital, was destroyed during the War of 1812. It was replaced in 1824 and now offers daily tours, featuring military demonstrations on Sundays.

**24. Adams National Historical Park**
Quincy, MA 02269
(617) 770-1175
www.nps.gov/adam

The park, comprising 10 acres in Quincy, Massachusetts, includes the building that was home to John Adams, America's second president, as well as to John Quincy Adams, the nation's sixth president, and the two houses that were the birthplaces of the two presidents. John Adams and his wife Abigail bought the house in 1781.

**25. Charleston Navy Yard**
Boston, MA 02129
(617) 242-5601
www.nps.gov/bost/

One of the 16 sites of the Boston National Historic Park, the Charleston Navy Yard dates from 1800. The historic frigate, the USS *Constitution* ("Old Ironsides") is docked here for public viewing. A museum interprets the history of "Old Ironsides" as well as other naval history.

**26. The Concord Museum**
Jct. of Cambridge Turnpike and Lexington Road
Concord, MA 01742
(508) 369-9609
www.concordmuseum.org

The museum exhibits Native American artifacts and items from the late 18th and early 19th centuries, such as Paul Revere's lantern, Ralph Waldo Emerson's personal effects from his study, Thoreau's belongings from Walden Pond, and examples of furniture and decorative arts.

**27. Lowell National Historic Park**
169 Merrimack Street
Lowell, MA 01852
(508) 459-1000
www.nps.gov/lowe

The park, which comprises 137 acres in Lowell, Massachusetts, commemorates the Industrial Revolution in America. Included here are historic 19th-century cotton textile mill complexes, over five miles of a canal network, and housing for the mill workers. The exhibits interpret the transition from a farm to a factory economy in the northeastern United States, immigrant labor history, and the development of industrial technology.

**28. Salem Maritime National Historic Site**
174 Derby Street
Salem, MA 01970
(508) 740-1660

The site consists of nine acres along the Salem waterfront, about twenty miles northeast of Boston, Massachusetts. Visitors can view the three remaining wharves—Derby Wharf with its lighthouse, Central Wharf, and Hatch's Wharf—out of the fifty busy wharves that once extended out into the harbor; the Custom House; the Scale House; the West India Goods Store; the Derby House; the Hawkes House; the Narbonne-Hale House. Salem merchants, ship owners, and sea captains grew wealthy through worldwide trade, but a decline set in with the 1807 embargo against trade with Britain and France, and the War of 1812 against Britain, and Salem never recovered.

**29. Springfield Armory National Historic Site**
One Armory Square
Springfield, MA 01105
(413) 734-8551
www.nps.gov/index.html

The Springfield Armory, the government arsenal which turned out the first American musket in 1795, was attacked on January 25, 1787, by Daniel Shays and his followers, who were rebelling against taxes they could not afford to pay. The rebellion was crushed by militiamen under the command of General William Shepherd. The 55-acre site features several buildings of the original armory complex, including the Main Arsenal Building, the Commanding Officer's Quarters, and the Master Armorer's House.

**30. Mackinac State Historic Parks—Colonial Michilimackinac**
102 W. Straits Avenue
Mackinaw City, MI 49701
(616) 627-5563
www.mackinac.com/historicparks

The park includes a reconstruction of Fort Michilimackinac, a French and British military outpost and fur-trading village founded in 1715, as well as 18th-century furnishings, and archeological and military collections.

**31. Mackinac State Historic Parks—Fort Mackinac and Mackinac Island State Park**
Mackinac Island, MI 49757
(906) 847-3328
www.mackinac.com/historicparks

The historic site of Fort Mackinac (1780-1895) includes 19th-century furnishings, Indian artifacts, and blacksmithing and military items.

**32. Stuart House City Museum**
Market Street
Box 1194
Mackinac Island, MI 49757
(906) 847-8181

The museum includes items related to the War of 1812, as well as records of the American Fur company's Fur Post, furs and pelts, Indian artifacts, and furnished rooms typical of the 1800s.

**33. Historic Daniel Boone Home and Boonesfield Village Lindenwood University**
1868 Highway F
Defiance, MO 63341
(314) 798-2005 and 798-2903
www.geocities.com/Athens/Parthenon/7109/

The historic house (1803-1810) was designed and built by Daniel Boone and patterned after his father's home in Pennsylvania. There is a guided tour through the historic village (1801-1850). Visitors can view authentic documents, furniture, and artifacts of the Boone family.

**34. Jefferson National Expansion Memorial**
11 North 4th Street
St. Louis, MO 63102
(314) 425-4465
www.nps.gov/jeff/

The memorial, comprising 91 acres on the west bank of the Mississippi River in St. Louis, Missouri, consists of Gateway Arch, the Museum of Westward Expansion, and the St. Louis Old Courthouse. The museum, located below the Arch, is as large as a football field and contains an extensive collection of artifacts, mounted animal specimens, an authentic Native American tipi, and an overview of the Lewis and Clark expedition of 1804-1806.

**35. Boxwood Hall Historic Site**
1073 East Jersey Street
Elizabeth, NJ 07201
(201) 648-4540

Boxwood Hall (c.1750), also known as Boudinot Mansion, once housed Elias Boudinot, a president of the Continental Congress and signer of the Treaty of Peace with Great Britain. George Washington visited the mansion on April 23, 1789, while en route to his inauguration in New York City.

**36. Ringwood State Park**
Ringwood, NJ 07456
(201) 962-7031

The park is located about 2 1/2 miles north of Ringwood, New Jersey, via Skyland Drive, CR 511, and Sloatsburg Road. Visitors to the park can view exhibits of the history of New Jersey's iron industry from 1740 to the 1920s, which can be found on the third floor of Ringwood Manor.

**37. General Jacob Brown Historical Society**
216 Brown Boulevard
Brownville, NY 13615
(315) 782-7650

The Historical Society Museum is housed in the 1811-1815 General Brown Mansion, and features collections of Brown furnishings, period pieces, dishes and cooking utensils, tools, weapons, and paintings, as well as Brown family memorabilia and research materials pertaining to the local history of Brownville and the War of 1812.

**38. Castle Clinton National Monument**
26 Wall Street
New York, NY 10005
(212) 344-7220

The monument, comprising one acre in Battery Park at the southern tip of Manhattan, includes a structure dating from 1811 that was one of several fortified military defense installations to protect New York City and its harbor against the possibility of British attack during the War of 1812.

**39. Federal Hall National Memorial**
26 Wall Street
New York, NY 10005
(212) 825-6990
www.nps.gov/feha/

The U.S. government began to function in New York's City Hall, renamed Federal Hall, on March 4, 1789. On April 30, 1789, George Washington took the oath of office as the nation's first president on the second-floor balcony of Federal Hall. In 1790 the federal government moved to Philadelphia; Federal Hall gradually fell into disrepair, and was finally demolished in 1812. The present building was built in 1942 to accommodate a U.S. customs house and then a subtreasury. Inside the building is a large bronze statue of George Washington, sculpted by John Quincy Adams Ward in 1883.

**40. Hamilton Grange National Memorial**
287 Convent Avenue
New York, NY 10031
(212) 283-5154

Hamilton Grange was the country estate that Alexander Hamilton, the nation's first Secretary of the Treasury, built for his wife Elizabeth and their five children. The house is in the process of being restored to its original appearance.

**41. John Jay Homestead State Historic Site**
400 Jay Street
Katonah, NY 10536
(914) 232-5969

The historic site museum was the home of U.S. chief justice and former New York state governor John Jay. Sixty-four of the original 760 acres are accessible to visitors. The federal-style country home contains period furnished rooms, American art from 1800-1830, and Jay family possessions.

**42. Schuyler Mansion State Historic Site**
32 Catherine Street
Albany, NY 12202
(518) 434-0834
www.nysparks.com

The Schuyler Mansion was the home of the noted Revolutionary War general and U.S. senator from New York, Philip Schuyler. His daughter Betsy married Alexander Hamilton in the house.

**43. New York Historical Society**
170 Central Park West at 77th Street
New York, NY 10024
(212) 873-3400
www.nyhistory.org

The New York Historical Society houses a museum, print room, and reference library. Its collections focus upon American history, New York history, and American fine arts and the decorative arts.

**44. New York Public Library**
42nd Street at Fifth Avenue
New York, NY 10017
(212) 930-0800

The New York Public Library features more than five million volumes in its research library, including specialized collections of American history.

**45. West Point Museum The United States Military Academy**
Bldg. 2110
West Point, NY 10996
(914) 938-2203 and 3590
www.usma.edu (selected site MUSEUM)

Exhibits at the West Point Museum trace the history of the Academy, established in 1802 by Congress to train military officers. The site was a vital fort during the Revolutionary War and also displays a monument dedicated to Civil War soldiers.

**46. Historic Latta Plantation**
5225 Sample Road
Huntersville, NC 28078
(704) 875-2312

The historic house museum includes an 1800 house with federal period furniture, decorative arts, agricultural artifacts, back country items, plantation outbuildings, working kitchen, and antique cooking utensils. In addition to the house, the site includes barns and a log house.

**47. Knife River Indian Villages National Historic Site**
Stanton, ND 58571
(701) 745-3309
www.nps.gov/knri

This site is part of the Lewis and Clark National Historic Trail. It comprises 1,758 acres near the confluence of the Knife and Missouri Rivers in west-central North Dakota, near the town of Stanton, and contains the remains of three Native American villages of the Mandans and Hidatsas. The Lewis and Clark expedition spent the winter of 1804-1805 near here.

**48. Perry's Victory and International Peace Memorial**
Put-in-Bay, OH 43456
(419) 285-2184
www.nps.gov/pevi/

Located on 26 acres in northern Ohio on the Lake Erie island of South Bass, near Sandusky and Port Clinton, the memorial commemorates Commodore Oliver Hazard Perry's victory on Lake Erie during the War of 1812, and the resulting international peace between the United States and Canada.

**49. Fort Clatsop National Memorial**
Astoria, OR 97103
(503) 861-2471

This site is part of the Lewis and Clark National Historic Trail. Located five miles southwest of Astoria, Oregon, near U.S. 101, it comprises 125 acres, and features a replica of the log fort built by the Lewis and Clark expedition during their encampment near the Pacific Ocean in the winter of 1805-1806. It was named for the Clatsops, a friendly local Native American tribe.

**50. Daniel Boone Homestead**
400 Daniel Boone Road
Birdsboro, PA 19508
(610) 582-4900

Situated on 579 acres, the site includes the 1730-1779 Boone House, smokehouse, barn, blacksmith shop, Bertolet log house, bake house, and Bertolet Sawmill. The museum includes collections of rural decorative arts, furniture, and agricultural and blacksmithing tools.

**51. Old Bedford Village**
Bedford, PA 15522
(814) 623-1156 or (800) 238-4347

Located one mile north of Bedford, Pennsylvania, on U.S. 220, 3/4 miles south of Exit 11 of the Pennsylvania Turnpike, this 40-building reconstruction of a village from the 1750-1850 period features demonstrations of crafts of the time such as tinsmithing, broom making, leather making, quilting, spinning, weaving, and woodworking.

**52. Deshler-Morris House**
5442 Germantown Avenue
Philadelphia, PA 19144

This 1750s home was built by the German immigrant David Deshler, after he had become a prosperous Philadelphia Quaker merchant. The house was leased by George Washington in 1793 when a yellow fever epidemic raged throughout Philadelphia, which was the nation's capital from 1790 to 1800.

**53. Robert Fulton Birthplace**
1932 Robert Fulton Highway
Quarryville, PA 17566
(717) 548-2755
members/aol/com/SLCHS/SLCHS.html

The site includes the house (c.1760) in which Robert Fulton was born. There are collections of period furniture and genealogical material.

**54. U.S. Brig Niagara, Homeport Erie Maritime Museum**
Bayview Commons
150 East Front Street
Erie, PA 16507
(814) 452-2744
www.brigniagara.org

This museum features the historic ship U.S. *Brig Niagara* (1813), which was commanded by Commodore Oliver Hazard Perry in the Battle of Lake Erie during the War of 1812. There are also exhibits pertaining to 19th-century sailing and regional maritime history.

**55. Hopewell Furnace National Historic Site**
2 Mark Bird Lane
Elverson, PA 19520
(610) 582-8773
www.nps.gov/hofu/index.html

This site, comprising 848 acres, is an example of a 19th-century rural iron plantation that operated from 1771, the year it was built by Mark Bird, to 1883. Among the buildings here are the blast furnace, casthouse, ironmaster's mansion, blacksmith shop, company store, charcoal cooling shed, barn, and tenants' quarters.

**56. Independence National Historical Park**
313 Walnut Street
Philadelphia, PA 19106
(215) 597-8974

Independence National Historical Park comprises 44 acres, mostly in downtown Philadelphia, and includes 26 historic properties associated with the American Revolution and the founding and development of the United States, such as Independence Hall, where the U.S. Constitution was crafted during the summer of 1787 and signed on September 17th. Other properties include the Afro-American Historical and Cultural Museum, the Army-Navy Museum, Congress Hall, the Betsy Ross House, the History Museum of Philadelphia, City Hall, the United States Mint, the Declaration House, Independence Square, and the Liberty Bell.

**57. Mercer Museum of the Bucks County Historical Society**
84 South Pine Street
Doylestown, PA 18901
(215) 345-0210
www.libertynet.org/bchs

Exhibits at Mercer Museum trace the pre-industrial history of the nation from colonization to the Civil War. More than sixty crafts and trades are represented by artifacts and implements from the 18th and 19th centuries.

**58. Pittsburgh Convention and Visitors Bureau**
4 Gateway Center, Suite 514
Pittsburgh, PA 15222
(412) 281-7711 or (800) 359-0758

The site of Pittsburgh was selected by George Washington during the Revolutionary War, and the town grew rapidly. In 1794, "Whiskey Rebels," farmers protesting the federal government's tax on whiskey, threatened to attack Pittsburgh. They dispersed without a fight at the approach of troops led by George Washington and Alexander Hamilton. Sites of interest include the Allegheny Observatory, the Carnegie Library of Pittsburgh, the Historical Society of Western Pennsylvania, the Pittsburgh Children's Museum, the Point State Park, and the Soldiers and Sailors Memorial Hall.

**59. Slater Mill Historic Site**
Roosevelt Avenue
Pawtuckett, RI 02865
(401) 725-8638
www.slatermill.org

This five-acre site, devoted to the origins of the industrial age in America, includes Slater Mill (1793), the first water-powered textile mill to successfully produce cotton yarn; Wilkinson Mill (1810), which housed a machine shop where textile machinery was built and repaired, and which produced cotton and woolen thread; and the Sylvannus Brown House (1758), the home of a millwright, which is furnished as it was in the early 1800s.

**60. Charles Pinckney National Historic Site**
1214 Middle Street
Sullivan's Island, SC 29482
(803) 881-5516
www.nps.gov/chpi

The site, consisting of 28 acres in Mount Pleasant, South Carolina, features brick foundations of structures dating from the time of Pinckney's ownership and a tidewater house dating from the 1820s. Charles Pinckney (1757-1824), an officer in the Revolutionary War, was one of the framers of the U.S. Constitution, served in the state assembly and four terms as governor of South Carolina, served in the U.S. House of Representatives and Senate, and was minister to Spain during Thomas Jefferson's administration.

**61. Shelburne Museum and Heritage Park**
US Route 7
Shelburne, VT 05482
(802) 985-3344
www.shelburnemuseum.org

The park includes 37 restored buildings housing collections of art, artifacts, and memorabilia depicting early New England life. Some of the structures are furnished 18th- and 19th-century houses, a jail, country store, schoolhouse, stagecoach inn, apothecary, blacksmith shop, and railroad depot.

**62. The Vermont Museum**
Pavilion Office Building
Montpelier, VT 05602
(802) 828-2291

The museum traces the history of Vermont, from the Native Americans to the present. Changing exhibitions feature different historical themes.

**63. Gunston Hall Plantation**
10709 Gunston Road
Mason Neck, VA 22079
(703) 550-9220
visit.gunstonhall.org/GunstonHall/

Gunston Hall (1755) was built by George Mason, author of the Virginia Declaration of Rights of 1776 and one of the authors of the U.S. Constitution. Designed by William Buckland, the main house features woodcarvings and English and American furnishings. Also on the grounds are outbuildings, including the dairy, kitchen, laundry, smokehouse, schoolhouse, and formal 18th-century-style gardens.

**64. The James Madison Museum**
129 Caroline Street
Orange, VA 22960
(540) 672-1776
www.gemlink.com/jmmuseum/

Museum collections include artifacts dealing with James and Dolley Madison and their family, and exhibits related to the Constitution, as well as 18th-century agriculture, farming, and transportation.

**65. Hugh Mercer Apothecary Shop**

Caroline and Amelia Streets
Fredericksburg, VA 22401
(703) 373-3362
www.apva.org

Opened in 1761, the apothecary features a drug room with curious bottles, ancient showcases, and yellowed ledgers; a sitting room; and a small library used by George Washington as an office. Demonstrations of 18th-century medical practices include leeching, cupping, bleeding, and herbal remedies.

**66. James Monroe Museum and Memorial Library**

908 Charles Street
Fredericksburg, VA 22401
(540) 654-1043
www.flstarweb.com/museum/tour

The museum includes collections of Louis XVI furniture used in the Monroe White House, personal costumes, jewelry, possessions of President and Mrs. James Monroe, manuscript collections, rare books, and U.S. presidential collection. The library inclues a 10,000-volume collections of books about Monroe's life and times, and 27,000 historic documents.

**67. Monticello, Home of Thomas Jefferson**

**Thomas Jefferson Memorial Foundation**

Route 53 and Thomas Jefferson Parkway
Charlottesville, VA 22902
(804) 984-9801
www.monticello.org

This imposing mansion was designed by Thomas Jefferson and was his home from 1769 to 1826. Exhibits include Jeffersonian furniture, memorabilia, art objects, manuscripts, books, and personal items.

**68. Mount Vernon Ladies' Association of the Union**

Mount Vernon, VA 22121
(703) 799-8650
www.mountvernon.org

Located at the end of George Washington Parkway South, George Washington's estate on the Potomac River has been restored to its 1799 appearance. This is where the Washington family settled in 1738 and George and Martha raised her two children after their marriage in 1759. The mansion and museum include such items as the bed where Washington died, and Washington's sword. Also on the grounds are the stables, kitchen, gardens, rebuilt greenhouses, slave quarters, and tomb of George and Martha Washington. The site has been preserved by the Mount Vernon Ladies' Association of the Union.

**69. The Rotunda, University of Virginia**
Charlottesville, VA 22902
(804) 924-7969 and 1019
www.virginia.edu/urelat/Tours/rotunda/rotunda.html

Thomas Jefferson exerted a major influence upon the architecture of Charlottesville. Here in 1819, he founded and designed the University of Virginia, with its Rotunda, pavilions, student rooms, and the lawn. Exhibits include material relating to the university's architectural history, prints and engravings of the grounds, and early-19th-century American furniture. Nearby is James Monroe's country estate, Ash Lawn, and Jefferson's own mansion, Monticello.

**70. George Washington Birthplace National Monument**
RR1, Box 717
Washington's Birthplace, VA 22443
(804) 224-1732
www.nps.gov/gewa

The monument is situated on 538 acres along the shore of Popes Creek in Virginia. Access from I-95 is by way of State Route 3, 38 miles east of Fredericksburg, Virginia. Washington was born and spent his childhood at this site, a recreation of Popes Creek Plantation, an 18th-century tobacco farm. Included here are the historic birthplace home area and colonial farm, as well as Washington family tombs.

**71. Lewis and Clark Interpretive Center**
Fort Canby State Park
Ilwaco, WA 98624
(360) 642-3029

Items related to Lewis and Clark are on display, along with coast artillery items and Coast Guard and lighthouse artifacts.

**72. Sacajawea Interpretive Center**
Sacajawea State Park
2503 Sacajawea Park Road
Pasco, WA 99301
(509) 545-2361

Collections include 7,000 B.C. to early 19th-century stone and bone tools of Columbia Plateau Indians, displays honoring the Lewis and Clark Expedition, and material pertaining to the culture of area Indians.

# INDEX